God's Plan
for Marriage

God's Plan for Marriage

by Stanley C. Brown

Stanley C. Brown

The Westminster Press
Philadelphia

Scripture quotations from the Revised Standard Version of The Holy Bible, Old Testament Section, Copyright 1952; New Testament Section, First Edition, Copyright 1946; New Testament Section, Second Edition, © 1972 by the Division of Christian Education of the National Council of the Churches of Christ in the U.S.A. Used by permission.

First Edition

PUBLISHED BY THE WESTMINSTER PRESS®
PHILADELPHIA, PENNSYLVANIA

PRINTED IN THE UNITED STATES OF AMERICA

9 8 7 6 5 4 3 2 1

Library of Congress Cataloging in Publication Data

Brown, Stanley C
  God's plan for marriage.

  1. Marriage. I. Title.
BV835.B74   253.5   77–6674
ISBN 0–664–24758–X

This book is dedicated to my parents, Bill and Marion Brown, who so loved me in all seasons that these thoughts and experiences could become a reality. They laid the foundation for my own love, joy, and peace. I trust the building on that foundation will bless many generations.

Contents

Part IV.   Living as a Family

Introduction

Recently, my wife Ruth and I celebrated twenty-five years of marriage. I don't find it getting any easier. I mean, life does not seem to turn into smooth sailing. Every year has its new challenges. We are at that period now where most of our children are gone, and that requires new goals and purposes for mom and dad. We've had them all with us on vacation. Our twenty-three-year-old daughter with husband and child were with us for over a week. Our twenty-one-year-old son was with us for the summer, digging ditches to fund himself beyond mom and dad. It was the summer before his college senior year, his last before being all on his own. Our sixteen-year-old daughter was with us, of course, with several groups of friends as houseguests. Our lives are made up of these relationships and the kaleidoscope of problems they provide with which to cope.

As we enter our late forties we have begun to accumulate a cluster of chronic health problems. We laugh at ourselves more often now. The other evening I realized that it had been a while since I looked closely at my wife's face as I have done for so many years, studying her eyes and facial features. We ended up dissolved in laughter because to focus at that close range we both had to put on our granny glasses.

I think we cry less now over our problems and more over sentimental things. Not that we have fewer problems, but crying never solved them. We cry over things we enjoy. We have learned to let go of some anxieties, I think. Life is freer in many ways, more mellow.

My family moved when I was in the fourth grade, and my new schoolroom included a girl with dark eyes who early caught my special attention. By the eighth grade we had discovered we could dance together better than with anyone else in our crowd. Since we were the same height, we walked together down the aisle at graduation from eighth grade to the familiar "Pomp and Circumstance." A little over a year later, when we were fifteen and just beginning our sophomore year of high school, we had our first date. I fell in love with her that night and we have been together ever since—six years of courtship, married when we were twenty-one, and finishing college together. We look back with gratitude to God for so many good years. We were privileged to do our youthful growing and identity-seeking together. We have loved each other a long time. We have been romantic through the years and thrived on it. We've been through much of life's changing scene, thinking at one time that we could not possibly live if one of us should die. We came through that to discover that for all of its sorrow the other would live on victoriously and hope to marry again.

We have found our life in the marriage relationship. It hasn't been handed to us on a silver platter. We have worked hard at our marriage and I suppose that is why the rewards have been so great. But ours isn't the only way, surely! One of the hardest battles our children have had to fight is getting over trying to repeat their parents' story. It's our story; it can't be everyone's. Where does fulfillment in life come, anyway? Is marriage the only way? Is a marriage like ours the best one?

These and other questions about marriage in today's world are the subjects of this book.

S.C.B.

PART ONE

God's Plan for Marriage

Chapter 1

A Love
for All Seasons

Loneliness is the first negative note in the Bible. Out across that newly ordered creation God's word spoke: "It is not good that the man should be alone; I will make a helper fit for him" (Gen. 2:18). This chapter is about God's plan to overcome that problem.

Plato tells a legend in which the original human beings were double what we are in size and strength. This made them arrogant and so the gods cut them in halves. According to the legend, real happiness comes when the two halves find and marry each other and complete their wholeness.

This same insight is more majestically told in the book of Genesis: "So God created man in his own image, in the image of God he created him; male and female he created them. And God blessed them, and God said to them, 'Be fruitful and multiply'" (Gen. 1:27–28). The older, more picturesque version is found in ch. 2: "Then the LORD God said, 'It is not good that the man should be alone; I will make him a helper fit for him.' . . . And the rib which the LORD God had taken from the man he made into a woman and brought her to the man. Then the man said, 'This at last is bone of my bones and flesh of my flesh. . . .' Therefore a man leaves his father and his mother and cleaves to his wife, and they become one flesh" (Gen. 2:18, 22–24).

It is as though a person is two separate parts, male and female, each part incomplete without the other. In each other, two persons recognize themselves and discover what is missing. Designed to complement each other, they build a united life together which brings meaning and creative force to them both. This is the supreme human relationship which becomes the path out of aloneness and into fellowship, out of lostness and into foundness, out of hating and into loving, out of self and into the other, out of misunderstanding and into understanding.

A priest-chaplain named Robert Griffin, at Notre Dame University, has written a book called *In the Kingdom of the Lonely God* (Paulist/Newman Press, 1973). In regard to the loneliness of the celibate life, he writes, "As a man without ties I am constantly on the lookout for a family to whom I can belong and who can, in turn, belong to me" (p. 64).

One day he was in the home of a family, thoroughly enjoying the feeling of belonging. He kicked off his shoes and was relaxing when the family dog, Alphie, came sniffing around and misused one of his shoes. Father Griffin noted that housebroken dogs don't do this to their owner families, and he took Alphie's act as a real rejection. "So," Griffin writes, "in my search for identity with family life, I hunt for my own lost childhood and the gleam of love necessary if any of us is to feel whole and authentic, as a reality that is grounded on God. Heaven is a time when all lost childhoods are recovered; until then, most of us must live with a restless sense of not belonging anywhere, and the news comes like a damp message in the shoe left by the watchdogs of life named Alphie." (*Ibid.*, p. 68.)

Rejection is met all through the Scriptures of the Old and New Testaments with God reaching out to persons through other persons. Interpersonal relationships seem to be God's plan for our fulfillment. In the Old Testament, God makes his approach through the patriarchs, the judges, the kings, the prophets, the husbands, the wives, and the children. In the context of these earthly relationships God makes himself known. He guides and teaches, woos and chastises. And out of it all, life takes on direction and purpose.

In the New Testament we meet again this personal God who loves the world, but never abstractly. He comes to us in human flesh, in the life of Jesus of Nazareth, a real person with whom persons then and now can become involved and find God in the relationship. This Son of God majored in defining God as Love. Love is never something we understand intellectually. It is experienced only in action, and that action involves human relationships. This greatest law of life is illustrated by Jesus as caring for the beaten stranger, getting up in the middle of the night and helping a neighbor, associating with people who admit their need no matter how low their reputation. When Jesus talks about the final judgment of God he illustrates it in terms of feeding the hungry, giving a drink to the thirsty, welcoming the stranger, clothing the naked, visiting the sick and imprisoned. Reaching out to each other at the points of our basic human needs: *this,* says the Bible from cover to cover, is what the meaning of life is all about.

Sometimes in the summer Ruth and the children would go to the mountains for a few weeks when I could not get away. When I was younger, such a separation would strike my heart with a loneliness that was sharp and acute. In my maturing years, there is still some of that, but something deeper sets in: a gnawing paralysis of motivation. A dull, heavy listlessness covers me like a pall and I feel as if the light within has gone out. Maybe that is the beginning of what it must be like to be widowed. God says, "This is not good!" Not right! Not what the divine will intended. Man stands in the lush garden. He tills and keeps it. He and God

have fellowship with each other. They walk together in the
cool of the evening, but somehow it is not complete. Adam
can praise God all day like the angels, but it is not enough.
The animals do his bidding, the natural resources and the
physical universe are his to use and develop; he can rise in
his imagination above the boundaries of earth and think like
a god. But for what? What is the purpose of it? God doesn't
need him! Here he is in this beautiful place, but alone. The
very word echoed pitifully among the green hills.

Adam couldn't understand all these feelings, but God
understood them. Man cannot be what God intended while
he is alone. Man's meaning is in his community. The image
of God is love—faith—hope: you cannot have these in isolation. None of us is a complete human being without the
I-Thou relationship where two persons complement and
serve and fulfill each other. If the hunger of our bodies for
food is the sign of our earthiness, the hunger of our souls
for love is the sign of our godliness. We need to be loved
and to give ourselves in love. The temptation is to love
ourselves so that we don't have to bother giving ourselves
to someone else. But self-love is not the answer to our
loneliness. It only deepens the terror and sets us running in
meaningless circles. We need above all else another person
to take us out of ourselves—a partner, a "Thou" to whom
we can devote our life and for whom we can lose ourselves.
Young people in their search for some way out of their
loneliness, in their anxiety over their boy-girl relationships,
in their seeking to find some kind of fulfillment in their
lives, reject their elders, who tell them their hunger can be
put off. It is the Spirit of God moving in them.

Can you imagine this vividly colored scene in Eden
where God paraded all the animals before Adam in review?
It was the first roundup and he put his brand on each of

them, gave each one a name. All the time he looked for a helpmate, but none was up to it. They all buckled under, all were subservient; no companionship or oneness was to be found with any in the lot.

Now see what God does during the afternoon siesta. Out of the man's very bone and flesh God builds a woman, another human being who is so like him that in her he recognizes himself. Yet she is different. The man and the woman are different from each other, in body and temperament and thought process. They complement each other, make up for what is lacking in the other, and, so serving each other, they both have a purpose for being alive. See the powerful meaning of the one coming from the rib of the other. Here is the polarity between us, the magnificent attraction of male and female which drives us to each other so that in community we may realize God's kind of love. In the one-flesh relationship of marriage we rediscover God's will for our wholeness and oneness. Man and woman don't "find" each other, they come to each other from each other, incomplete as long as they are separate, brought together by God himself. Our souls sing with Adam as we join in his shout of joy, "This at last is bone of my bones and flesh of my flesh; she shall be called *ishshah* (Woman), because she was taken out of *ish* (Man)" (Gen. 2:23).

In the next verse we are told that paradise is where "a man leaves his father and his mother and cleaves to his wife, and they become one flesh" (Gen. 2:24). If man's first assignment is to rule the creation, it seems that his second assignment is to take the loneliness out of other people's lives—not to reject them as the dog did Father Griffin, but to embrace them as part of the family.

It is no wonder all through the New Testament the Kingdom of God, or Paradise Regained, is spoken of as that union between Christ the Bridegroom and the community of believers the Bride. "Lost childhood recovered," Father Griffin? No, childhoods can be pretty lonely. Rather, the perfect marriage where each partner is fulfilled, completed, made whole. Husband and wife are vastly different from parent and child. God calls for leaving parents behind, putting away childish things, and going on to deeper relationships.

James Baldwin wrote a play called *The Amen Corner*. It is set among the Negroes of Harlem, but its message is not simply racial. A wife has left her husband, to pursue a career as an evangelist. Years later the estranged father, named Luke, a jazz trombonist, shows up dying of tuberculosis. His son, David, learns for the first time that his father did not desert them but that his mother walked out on Luke. The horror of what she did is movingly revealed when Luke tells David that the most terrible time in a man's life is when everything that has held him together is suddenly gone and he can't find it. He says: "Then that man start going down. If don't no hand reach out to help him, that man goes under." Luke explains how a man can survive the most drastic losses *if* he has one thing: "I don't believe no man . . . [can survive] without somebody loved him. Somebody *looked* at him, looked *way* down in him spied him way down there and showed him to himself—and then started pulling, a-pulling of him up—so he could live." (James Baldwin, *The Amen Corner*, pp. 43f.; The Dial Press, Inc., 1968.)

When David asks his father why the wonderful jazz music he has created did not satisfy him, did not keep him happy and proud, Luke sadly replies: "Music ain't kissing. Kissing's what you want to do. Music's what you *got* to do, *if* you got to do it. Question is how long you can keep up with the music when you ain't got nobody to kiss. You know, the music don't come out of the air, baby." (*Ibid.*, p. 44.)

That is so true. No meaningful, creative force just comes out of the air. It comes from caring. It comes from human relationships of love which lend meaning and purpose to life.

No wonder our Lord Jesus Christ made it so clear that marriage is not something in which to dabble! This is not a human contract or an adventure in emotions and economics. This is a sacrament which reveals the purposes of life itself. One marriage I refused to perform was for a couple who calmly announced that they meant to enter marriage on a trial basis. Marriage is a spiritual covenant which works only on a basis of lifelong faithfulness.

In the famous and often misunderstood fifth chapter of Ephesians, the great apostle describes the marriage relationship by comparing it to Christ's relationship with his church. When we see the life of Jesus serving the needs of others, when we see him go to the cross sacrificing his own desires for our needs, yet finding his meaning and purpose and victory in the sacrifice, then we see the love which God intends to animate the marriage relationship. "Be subject to one another out of reverence for Christ. Wives, be subject to your husbands, as to the Lord. . . . Husbands, love your wives, as Christ loved the church and gave himself up for her." (Eph. 5:21, 25.)

So marriage becomes a living prototype, two persons working at becoming one and finding between them the forgiveness, the sacrificing love, the servanthood, and the fulfillment which puts life together. Of course, this vision of marriage requires the presence of God in it. If it is to be a reflection of the Kingdom of God, then God himself must be King in that relationship of husband and wife.

In the Philippine Islands, Charles Lindbergh led a National Geographic expedition in a study of the Tasaday tribe. The members of this tribe are genuine cave dwellers, lost to civilization in the jungles of Mindanao. Here for the first time modern man is able to study prehistoric man in his natural setting. The Tasadays marry and stay together as couples all their lives. There is no divorce or mate-sharing. They say, "We marry so we have a companion to share with." When there is a marriage ceremony it is held in the opening of their main cave while the group gathers around the new couple and says, "Good! Good! Good!" It has the ring of God's creation in it. Marriage is not just one option offered by man's many-splendored culture. It is the Way of Life that is built in from the beginning as God's will for our fulfillment on the earth.

So many factors complicate the picture today that some people are suggesting that marriage is outmoded. From where we stand we have to consider the third chapter of Genesis along with the second. The fact is that we are living not in the Garden of Eden, but in the world as it is pictured in Genesis the third chapter. We are living in a world that has fallen away from intimacy with God and has lost the paradise which God intended. We find homosexuality acknowledged and widespread because so many aberrations in family life have stamped some children with abnormal fears and roles to play which never do bring real fulfillment. Women's liberation surfaces again in our time because men for so long have put women down to a level that God never intended. Eve rises in rebellion, and for some the pendulum swings far to the other extreme. So, the "new morality," which is really the old immorality, comes bounding back in the guise of new and intriguing life-styles, putting the stamp of approval on adultery and completely ignoring the fact that sex is vastly more than a physical meeting. Sexual hunger is the pilgrimage toward our deepest needs for an ultimate relatedness. It is a key to fulfillment and trust and oneness. That psychological security can be met only in the one-partner plan.

Chapter 2

An Alternative to Marriage

We do not exist apart and isolated. The only place we can find fulfillment, satisfaction, and meaning in life is in relationship to another person. The brokenness and tragedy in our lives come from our alienation, our separation, our lack of relationship. This is much of what is behind the youth revolution. It's not a rebellion against God or family or country; it's rebellion against hypocrisy and phoniness, inhumanness and irrelevancy and automation! It is a crying out of human souls for honest relationships and for the fulfillment of human potential.

From the beginning, Jesus' ministry was one of deep personal human relationships. He always got right in among people, identified with them, and shared their burdens. Out of the experience they found rest for their souls. Something always happened in that exchange of heart with heart, soul with soul, mind with mind, touch with touch—something beautiful and exciting which those involved called "God," something which changed them forever after.

Right now, imagine yourself in an elevator. Others have gotten on with you. Are you touching anyone? Do you look anyone in the eye? Does anyone speak? You ride close together, yet worlds apart—uncomfortable, silent. You can hardly wait to get out. At one floor still more people get on, but everyone stands scrunched up so no one has to touch anyone else.

On a downtown street we are stampeded or on the freeway we are surrounded by living, breathing human beings, but we might as well all be machines. At work, at recreation, people are all around us, but great invisible walls rise between us. We have a good excuse, of course. We are busy, we are pursuing hard work, efficiency, success, bigness, progress. These are the gods we've fashioned. We go year after year in factory, office, shop, or neighborhood without meeting anyone who takes an interest in us as persons. We associate with companions we never really know and who never know us. With whom do we share our secret burdens? Where in the speeding crowd do we look into another's eyes? Where do we break out of this unbelievable spiritual solitude? If ever you wanted to put your finger on the curse, here it is: lack of deep, intimate relationship with another.

We have seen that God has provided for this profound need for spiritual, physical, emotional, and intellectual intimacy. "It is not good that man should be alone; I will make him a helper fit for him" (Gen. 2:18). When the other person was formed out of man's rib it was a beautiful symbol saying that neither is complete without the other, that there can be no fulfillment alone. God brought the two persons together, and a shout of joy went up that echoes in all souls: "This at last is bone of my bones and flesh of my flesh" (Gen. 2:23).

But what about the unmarried person?

An unmarried minister advertised for a handyman around the parsonage. The next morning a young man rang the doorbell. The minister invited him in and began a barrage of questions. "Can you start a fire and have breakfast ready by six in the morning?"

"I'm sure I can do that," said the young man.

"Can you polish the floors, wash and dry dishes, and cook?"

With that the young man put in, "Look, Reverend, I came here to see about getting married, but if marriage is going to be like that, you can count me out!"

There are some persons in our society who are counted out of marriage. What about the person who married unsuccessfully and is divorced? Where is fulfillment for the person who chooses not to marry, whatever the reason may be? What about the person who is homosexual? What does the Christian gospel have to say to the problem of homosexuality in our society? A distinct percentage of people have this problem, and the Lord Christ must be relevant for their situation too. Psychologists and medical people still debate the degree to which a person is born with homosexual tendencies and the degree to which these tendencies are created by the environment. The Bible refers to the problem in a judgmental way. It was prevalent in Canaanite times and in Greek times. It was included in pagan worship and seen in the breakdown of civilizations. There is no soft spot for the practice anywhere in the Bible. But to end the discussion at that point is to cling to the law and miss the spirit of the law. Laws are designed to express principles in a given time. Principles do not change. Laws have to change to make the principle relevant in a new situation. Homosexuality is a case in point.

Scholars agree that the Bible writers knew little or nothing about confirmed homosexuals. The subject is always dealt with in the Bible as a promiscuous activity of moral decay, totally against a person's natural inclinations. They did not understand that in some cases this could be a person's natural inclination. It wasn't until about 1890 that the confirmed homosexual person was recognized. Only since then has our knowledge begun to deal with hormones and body chemistry and the psychological shaping of children, especially in the home where there is not a healthy masculine figure. The question we Christians face is not how to be judgmental so much as how to mediate the love of God to the homosexual torn with conflict and torment. I have counseled for long hours with men and women whose childhoods were so disturbed that their homosexual life-styles came as no surprise to me.

Where do these people who do not conform to the pattern of marriage find fulfillment and fit into society—not just the persons with homosexual problems but the persons who choose not to be married, who are divorced, and who are widowed?

Many know the sorrow of losing a husband or wife through death. The sorrow is theirs alone to bear, except for that great outpouring of sympathy and support from those who care. But the sorrow of spinsterhood receives little consolation. How many spinsters who seem in public to have overcome their disappointment will dissolve into tears in private. Most women who see the years go by and their hopes for marriage evaporating experience a deep sorrow resurfacing again and again. They conceal their sorrow, pretend not to wince at the jokes, the allusions to sex, or the flippant talk of being better off without the responsibility of a husband and a child. It is not just being deprived of fulfillment in sex and motherhood. It is the loneliness, the empty aloneness, which is so contrary to God's plan. Despite the gallant *Playboy* image shown by many unmarried men, the bachelor is usually very lonely, doubting and unhappy within. Married men score highest in job-satisfaction ratings and in good feelings about themselves, higher than either single men or single women. In college my wife had a housemother who would introduce herself with these words, *"Miss Merris, by choice!"* There was a look in her eye that defied anyone to make light of her status in life. Good show, Miss Merris!

One evening in a Bible class I was comparing our relationship to God with a love affair. Our need to work at it, to grow in it, and our longing to be with him reminded me of the days I was courting my wife. Nothing could keep me home. Tramping through snow and subzero weather, I would hold my rendezvous with her. It had all the elements of a worship service—the singing around the piano, the offerings I brought in the form of gifts, the dressing up to look my best, the serious hours of confession and soul-searching together, the praise and glory and honor I would express to her. In this context our love not only grew but God himself was revealed to us, he who is Love.

Upon reaching the end of that line of thought, I paused. The class was silent and pensive. A dear spinster, a retired teacher, spoke out: "I want to tell you something." Her voice was somewhat emotional. She spoke slowly, not at all her usual, bouncy, joyous self. All eyes turned to her. "I'm the only one here who isn't married. I went with a fellow for seven years, and we were engaged for six of those years. One night he said to me, 'I worship you,' and from then on I had nothing to do with him."

There was a pause. She seemed to be struggling again with her concern over idol worship and her love for this man. She continued: "Your saying all this brought it back. One night I called him up and said it was all off!" She paused. There had been pathos in her voice, and the class was electrified by this confession. We were all close from months of study together, but we were not prepared for this depth of self-revelation. "Seven years." She paused again, her voice trailing off. "Kind of sad."

After class, with a trace of tears, she went on to tell me how neither of them had ever married. He had died just the past year. Now this new insight: she had been wrong. His statement to her about worship in the context of their love for each other was not as off center as she had believed. In her almost stunned look I saw the lost years, the lost opportunity for fulfillment, and it was overwhelming.

Remember that the principle behind marriage is relationship. True enough, the male-female union is God's created plan. But when our sinful ways so boggle the normal plan, what do we do? Are these unmarried the damned? Is there no place for persons trapped by a fallen society? Are they barred from the Kingdom of God forever by the sins of the fathers, or do these persons also have a place in the family of God?

At one point Jesus said, in effect, anyone who saves or hoards his life will lose it (Mark 8:35 and parallels). This is one of the highest principles of life. It is true in marriage. It is true out of marriage. There is far too much emphasis today on self-fulfillment and self-realization. It is time we realized again that these are by-products which come when we concentrate on self-extension. In Christian marriage or outside of it, the key is to invest oneself in human relationships. How many lonely persons are waiting for you to get over your fear of being involved?

To have the courage to do this, not to fear this closeness with others, not to be afraid that you are going to lose your identity in the relationship, you must be clear about your own identity. It is the identity as a son or a daughter of God that the church has to offer the world. Good news! You are Christ's! Now that you know who you are and that you have infinite value, you can afford to lose yourself in relation-

ships. Now you are ready to extend yourself to a society that
is so troubled it needs the spiritual penicillin of those who
care.

There are so many lonely people who wait for our relatedness: our older relatives, parents without partners, single
adults separated from their families, older people with no
children nearby, adolescents alienated from their homes,
children who have lost one or both of their parents. The list
is long. The church can become the extended family, a
need-satisfying fellowship which provides love, caring, and
roots for uprooted, lonely people. What a joyous discovery
we make in Jesus Christ that the most important family is the
human family, which makes every person we meet a rela-
tive.

When I was young, we used to sing an old hymn about
the Kingdom of God called "Dwelling in Beulah Land."
Many years later in my studies I discovered that "Beulah"
is the Hebrew word for "married." The hymn compares the
delights of being married to the ecstasy of living in the
Kingdom of God. It praises God for that mountaintop experience which has joys and abundance unlimited, and shouts
with ecstasy, "For I am dwelling in Beulah Land." One
morning during a devotional time I found verses in Isaiah
that must have been the inspiration behind that old hymn:
"You shall no more be termed Forsaken, and your land
shall no more be termed Desolate; but you shall be called
My delight is in her, and your land [shall be called] Married
(Beulah); for the LORD delights in you, and your land shall
be married. . . . And as the bridegroom rejoices over the
bride, so shall your God rejoice over you" (Isa. 62:4–5).

The Christian married and the Christian unmarried find
their lives in knowing that God rejoices over them as a
groom over his bride. In Christ none of us is unmarried or

alone, and our charge is to take this good news and demonstrate it to all the lonely world.

Janet was ten years old and was already at the church when I arrived each Sunday at eight o'clock. She stayed all morning, two services and Sunday school. She sat on the front pew all by herself and kept her eyes fixed on me. Naturally my heart went out to her. We would talk before and after worship. She told me that her mother and stepfather were usually gone. Three teen-age brothers looked after her, but she was pretty much on her own. Sunday she would rise and dress and leave home without breakfast. During the week I would see her on the streets, often at dusk. She always smiled. She was always alone. Somehow she looked as if she always expected a "no" from life. Often she would ask to read books in the church library. Eventually she sang in our children's choir. I tried to visit in the apartment but never found anyone at home. Then one Sunday she handed me a note on her way out. It was carefully folded and I put it in my pocket to read later. When I got home I remembered it. I took it out and opened it and read: "I love you. I am moving. Your love, Janet." The next day I went by the apartment. It was locked up tight; the shades were drawn. It was too late, they had gone. I wondered what would become of Janet. Did she come to know Christ there with us? Did we go far enough to relate to her? Were the congregation and the choir and Sunday school enough? Or did we fail her? Were we too busy to take the time she needed? I told this story to my congregation, and afterward three people spoke to me with tears in their eyes. One was her Sunday school teacher, who said, "I never called on Janet." Another was the youth fellowship president, who said, "I lived upstairs from her." And the third was my wife, who said: "Three times she came to play with Beth, but it was right at suppertime and I sent her away. I could have invited her in."

How many others are there whose hearts are hungry, whose souls are lonely, whose spirits are blocked and infirm? How many are there who need us, the church, to be sensitive to them? The home is not a reality for many people in this day when families are breaking up and so many people are alone. Mary, the mother of Jesus, saw her home breaking up. She looked up into her son's eyes when she heard his voice: "Woman, behold, your son!" Then she turned to look at John, and Jesus said to him, "Behold, your mother!" John reports, "And from that hour the disciple took her to his own home" (John 19:26–27). Mary felt his touch at her elbow. She would go now. She would not look again; it was the end. As John led her down the hill she did not yet know that this was really the beginning. Yet to come was the upper room, when he would return in victory and live among his followers century after century. But she hadn't experienced that yet, and many people we meet have not yet experienced it.

That picture of the disciple leading the brokenhearted Mary down the hill and into the intimacy of his family circle is a picture of the church at its best. The church is a network of personal relationships healing the brokenness of all comers. The gospel must be expressed in relationships. Together in the church we get a taste of what heaven is all about. This should happen to some degree in everything we do together as Christians.

Chapter 3

When Marriage Fails

One October afternoon we drove fifty beautiful miles along the Aegean Gulf from Athens to Corinth. Here on a narrow isthmus the trade routes crossed which brought wealth to that ancient city. Here the famous Corinthian pillar was given to the world. We walked among the ruins of the Temple to Apollo and over the rubble of the great marketplace. We looked up and saw that massive rock which overshadows the place, the Acrocorinth. Every Greek city has this upper, fortified temple area. There on the Acrocorinth we could see the massive ruins of the Temple of Aphrodite where a thousand slave priestesses combined religion with prostitution, turning Corinth into the world's biggest brothel.

The Greek empire was conquered by Rome. Roman society was founded on the home. Morality was so high in Roman culture that for the first five hundred years of the Roman commonwealth not one single divorce was recorded. In conquering the Greek empire, Rome also absorbed the Greek culture. Greek immorality began to infiltrate the Roman Empire, and divorce became as common as marriage. It was about that time in history that Rome collapsed and was destroyed.

When we look at history we see dark signs of warning. It seems that anarchy in the family precedes anarchy in the state. Pick any declining civilization and see if adultery and divorce are not rampant. When marriage decays, the whole society decays with it.

The Master, Jesus Christ, knew that marriage was just this serious. Note this passage from his Sermon on the Mount: "It was also said, 'Whoever divorces his wife, let him give her a certificate of divorce.' But I say to you that every one who divorces his wife, except on the ground of unchastity, makes her an adulteress; and whoever marries a divorced woman commits adultery" (Matt. 5:31–32).

When Jesus uttered those words they were an incredible novelty, because a woman at that time had no rights of her own. Divorce was simple. A man merely wrote a letter dismissing her as his wife and sent her away. One day in Jerusalem the Pharisees were testing Jesus, as they often did, trying to get him to contradict the law of Moses. They asked, "Is it lawful to divorce one's wife for any cause?" (Matt. 19:31). Jesus took them back, before Moses and the laws, to the very order of creation, where man and woman were created for a lifelong, one-flesh union. The Pharisees asked him why Moses allowed divorce. Jesus said it was an allowance for sin but that was not God's plan from the beginning. Then our Lord adds that statement which is so hard for us to assimilate: "And I say to you: whoever divorces his wife, except for unchastity, and marries another, commits adultery" (Matt. 19:9). These words hit us hard, because they stand in such sharp contrast to the situation today.

One of the keys to understanding what Jesus is saying in these passages is to realize that he is not laying down laws for the general public. We get confused about this. Remember, the essence of the gospel is that we are now under grace and no longer under the law. The laws that a society lives by have to reflect the capacity of the people to keep them.

The law always compromises the ideal. The Sermon on the Mount, you will see from its introduction, is spoken not to the masses that followed Jesus but to the disciples. It is a description of life among those who share in the Kingdom of God. It is not the expectation for society in this world apart from Jesus Christ. This is a basic point in our understanding the teachings of Jesus. Only those who have the help of the Spirit of Christ can accept Christ's standard of living. Only the Spirit of Christ can enable the love and the sacrifice, the forgiveness, and the caring which marriage demands if it is to be what God intended. This is exactly why it is not enough to say, "I accept the ethics of the Kingdom of God, but I cannot be bothered to commit my life to Jesus Christ and all of that." Ethics alone have no power. Jesus, a great and good man, Jesus, the teacher, has no power except to be an example we can never equal. It is Jesus the Son of God whose living Presence makes the ethic come alive in me and for me. Without the power of God, my marriage can never be what God intended it to be. Jesus communicates that power of God when we believe in him.

Instead of legalisms, Jesus was speaking of a way of life in personal relationship with God. A law is rigid and impersonal; a law does not know you but is superimposed on you from the outside. A way of life, on the other hand is understood within the context of a real situation. Jesus sets forth the all-encompassing way called Love. It speaks to every situation from the inside and fulfills the law. Remember Augustine's statement, "Love God, and do as you please." Unfortunately, for the most part we are not committed body and soul to the way of love exemplified in Jesus, so laws are required to make life workable in society.

The way of love applies to marriage like this: God creates the community between a male and a female known as "marriage." This act of God in marriage is not subject to recall any more than the other acts of creation, like the earth and the stars. It is part of the natural order, too deep for human tampering. God is a third party in any marriage, participating in this new community. That is a fact beyond our choice. For us to break this created act of God is to do something profoundly evil. The result is indelible, like having one's legs cut off.

Divorce is never the will of God. Sometimes when all the forces of medicine and psychiatry and the church have tried to cure sickness in a marriage and it has proved incurable, divorce is the only way out. But when this happens it is always a concession to man's weakness. As Jesus said, when they questioned why Moses allowed for divorce, it was "for your hardness of heart . . . but from [creation] it was not so." Let's get over this idea that divorce is a way out of trouble or that it solves a problem. It may be the only action possible but it doesn't solve the problem. When the marriage is torn, something terrible happens, something unbalanced and wrong, like the breaking of a person's bones or the suffocation of one's breath. There are lacerations and wounds and the blood runs out. As in the crucifixion, God's heart is in this; God's heart is broken, too.

Divorce is an admission of sin. It can never be said that divorce rights the wrong. It only admits the wrong. When the courts dissolve the marriage they only legalize the present facts: that there is no marriage. The two have divorced themselves! Either they have destroyed the creation of God, the one-flesh union, or it was never real in the first place. How often persons come into marriage for fortune or fame or feelings, but never because God brought them together. Their souls were never joined and their marriage was as much a sin as their divorce. This teaching is hard for us to accept, especially today when society is fast convincing itself that divorce is really acceptable. Most divorced persons have perfectly good reasons why it had to be and they don't want to be called sinners. They prefer to be called "victims." But Christ is very clear: God's will is the indissolubleness of marriage. Divorce is always the admission that God's will has been broken. This point is so difficult to "hear" that it needs to be said again in a slightly different way. Divorce is disharmony and separation between two human beings. By definition, disharmony and separation are sin. There are many legal marriages that never have achieved the one-flesh union described in the Bible. When we speak of "one-flesh union" this is a reference not simply to a physical joining but to that deep soul entwined with soul, fulfilling each other and taking away loneliness. Many earthly marriages have never developed that kind of union, and the separation or disharmony has been present all along. What agony there is deciding whether to continue the farce and the harm it does or to dissolve the family and leave the wounds deep and permanent on all the members.

God has a beautiful plan! He gave me this human being to love and to serve at whatever the cost to myself. This marriage partner is not just to perform functions for me! If all she is to me is a means of sexual release or a money earner or a housekeeper or a social asset, then when she no longer performs these functions where is the marriage? This is the reason behind so much divorce. Two persons marry each other in order to get certain functions performed. But God intends marriage to bind person to person to the depths of their being, in a relationship of love and service until death.

These principles need to be considered from the perspective of three groups of people. The first group is composed of those who are not yet married, but are dating. I believe in love at first sight; I do not believe in marriage at first sight. It takes time for the two to know if they are really the right persons for each other. It takes time for God to create a marriage. This is why short courtships are often danger-ous. The two see each other only in the glamourous, care-free, and fun times. In marriage the glamour fades at the kitchen sink, and long nights with a sick baby are not care-free. Are you so suited for lifelong marriage that you will weather the days when money is a problem, when you are tired and weary, when the world and teen-age children put a constant strain on your relationship? How many seeds of sorrow are sown on the wedding day because the two are not emotionally ready to make the total commitment they now verbalize in their vows. Be sure that you do not marry out of insecurity. Be sure that you do not marry to escape from your parents. Be sure that you do not marry on the rebound from a love affair that failed. Be sure that you do not marry for a hundred other wrong reasons. Let God be part of your decision to marry. Spend time in prayer, seek-ing his guidance. Be sure to consult with your pastor as soon as you make your decision, or before. He can help you both to determine if you are ready for marriage and help you to prepare for it.

One bride was so nervous on the night of the rehearsal that the minister gave her a formula to help calm her down. He said: "When you begin that procession down the aisle, remember it's the aisle you have walked down all your life, as you've been raised in this church. Concentrate on the aisle. When you get halfway down you will look up and see the altar before which you have worshiped since you were a child. Concentrate on that altar. When you get two thirds of the way down you will see *him,* the one to whom you have pledged your faith and whom you know so well. Concentrate on *him,* and that will get you down there." The night of the wedding the bride was completely composed as she came down the center aisle, except that those near her heard her muttering between clenched teeth, "Aisle . . . altar . . . him; aisle . . . altar . . . him."

You who are anticipating marriage, be sure that you accept each other, warts and all. Don't enter marriage thinking that you will alter the undesirable things in your mate later on. Take each other as you are forever, or don't do it.

Secondly, a word to those who are married now, especially those whose marriage is not what they want it to be. There are many distress signals in the marriage relationship: sarcastic digs at each other, sudden spirited clashes, a loss of common interests, apathy, constant absences from the home, and most deadly of all, that breakdown of communication where the intimacy of the depth relationship withers and dies. This failure of love can grow like a creeping paralysis over the years. It can shatter the lives of any couple who do not keep close to the God of love and do not work at the practical matters of their relationship. It is painful to struggle through together to deeper levels of understanding. It is tempting to escape the pain and quit trying to reach out for each other. The great tragedy is that often when the pain of self-discovery is most acute and the two realize that they must change or perish, they call it off and break the relationship.

The first step in making a good marriage is refusing to consider divorce as an option. Pastors should use every possible resource in counseling. I am amazed at the number of couples who come to pastors for help after it is too late. Months and even years of strife have already gone by. Don't wait to seek help. Pray together. Put Jesus Christ at the center of your marriage. Concentrate on him, not on your feelings. If your partner won't do this, you can. Your partner's refusal is no excuse for you to leave Christ out. Christ's love is self-giving; it is constant with gentleness, joy, kindness, patience, and self-control, which will save the day if anything can.

Martin Luther put this all down into the commonplace, as he usually did. He is speaking for the husband, but it translates both ways. He wrote: "The best way to prevent divorce and other discord is for everyone to learn patience in putting up with the common faults and troubles of his station in life and to put up with them in his wife as well, knowing that we can never have everything just right, the way we would like to have it. Even the condition of your own body can never be any different or better. You have to put up with the many kinds of filth and discomfort that it causes you every day. . . . This only increases your concern and love for your body; you wait on it and wash it, and you endure it and help in every way you can. Why not do the same with the spouse whom God has given you, who is an even greater treasure and whom you have even more reason to love? . . . As Christ continually bears with us in his kingdom and forgives us all sorts of faults, so we should bear and forgive one another in every situation and in every way." (*Luther's Works,* Vol. 45: *The Christian in Society II,* p. 19; Muhlenberg Press, 1962.)

Finally, a word to those who have been divorced. Don't allow yourself to spend one minute in placing blame for the failure. *Every* person must acknowledge, "I am guilty of sin." We have *all* failed to be controlled by the love of God. Divorce is one horrible manifestation of sin. There are plenty of others. Many persons who remain married live in sin the world knows nothing about; but God knows. So to the divorced person I would say, we are all sinners. This is the hour to acknowledge our common guilt and to discover together that God is with us, that he wants to redeem us, and that life can begin again. Don't take the route of blame, either taking or giving it. Rather, accept the love of Jesus Christ and let him change you: change your weaknesses into strengths, your fears into confidence, your insecurity into assurance, your anger into peace and love.

As for remarriage, Christ laid down a principle and a way of life, not a law. Divorce breaks the order of creation. For divorced persons to remarry compounds the sin *if* there is no repentance: if nothing in them has really changed; if there has been no rebirth; if the new marriage also is outside of God's order of creation. But let me say again that we are under grace, not under the law. When a divorced person has experienced forgiveness, received it and given it, entered into a new relationship with God, and allowed God to create this new marriage, then remarriage is made holy by God.

Some years ago Jane came to my office. She had deserted her husband and her small son to run three states away with another man. Now she carried his child. All the confusion of it had come home to her sick heart. Soaked through on a rainy afternoon, she picked a pastor at random to whom she could cry out her agony and despair. We both agreed that her marriage was undoubtedly beyond repair. But none of us can second-guess God. Jane surrendered herself, soul and body, unborn child, child at home, husband, boyfriend, future. She surrendered it all to Jesus Christ. She promised to wait for what He would do.

In three months her husband had forgiven her and sent for her to come home. Later he adopted her child as his own. The order of God's creation was restored and Jane's new-found love in Christ was so powerful that her husband also surrendered his life to Jesus. Years later she wrote to me: "The more I learn, the more there is to learn about myself and about being really alive in each moment—that moment which is really all we have to live. . . . It is my fond hope that if your travels ever bring you along this road, . . . [we will renew] a friendship that in its inception was all yours in the giving, all mine in the taking. Life has finally brought me to the enjoyment of being the giver too, and that's been a joyous discovery."

That *is* the great discovery, to come out of the storm of our sin and broken relationships, turn it all over to Jesus Christ, and watch him create love, marriage, a home, and a new life.

PART TWO

Working at Marriage

Chapter 4

Be Mine

What is your earliest memory of Valentine's Day? Ruth and I were thinking back and for us it is a memory of the yearly party in our grade-school classroom. We took valentines for everybody in the room and deposited them in a big decorated box. It was like casting ballots for popularity. Someone was appointed to be the mailman, and at the close of a restless and exciting day the big box was opened. The valentines were distributed to their addressees, and the teacher provided cupcakes. The next stage in this drama was to compare statistics with our friends. "How many did you get?" "Well, I got fifteen. How many did *you* get?" When we arrived home we would spread them out on the living room floor and go over the names, trying to figure who in the class did not bother to send us one. The head count was always made more difficult because several valentines would be unsigned. That of course was the tradition in the first place.

Valentine's Day apparently had its origin in Roman paganism. There was an ancient belief that in the southern climates the birds mated on February 14 and the springtime fancy of boys for girls was expressed in a festival celebrating love. The names of young women were put into a box and drawn out by the young men in a lottery. The name a man drew was to be his sweetheart for the next year. He had to take the bitter with the sweet. The outgrowth of this was the sending of affectionate greetings and gifts to the one you love on this particular day of the year. If you were a secret admirer, your gift or letter was unsigned. It happened that in A.D. 270 a Christian bishop by the name of Valentine was martyred on the day of this festival, February 14. When he was designated a saint his day of martyrdom became a feast day in the church. As so often happens, the pagan and the Christian mingled. Christians began to exchange cards expressing their love on St. Valentine's Day. Parents and children, as well as sweethearts, would exchange gifts.

The familiar picture of the heart and the plea to "Be mine" still speak to us of the universal experience we call "falling in love." It is important to consider what the Christian faith has to say about it. Longfellow wrote, "There is nothing holier in this life of ours than the first consciousness of love—the first fluttering of its silken wings—the first rising sound of breath of that wind which is so soon to sweep through the soul, to purify or to destroy."

Falling in love is a complex, total experience. It is that all-consuming desire to reach out and draw the other person to yourself. It is a longing for total oneness. It is not just the animal sexual drive. We shall call that "Venus," as they did in ancient times. Venus is only part of Eros, the Greek word for human love. This powerful desire for the beloved is not aimed just at sensual pleasure; that much alone is Venus. Eros is less specific. It is directed to the beloved's total person. "Be mine" is a request for the body, the mind, the soul, the hopes, the dreams, the memories, of that total person. Love always sweeps us up with a total preoccupation. It has the highest and noblest intentions; it wants to do anything for the welfare of the beloved. Love is caught up in the moment and cannot make any long-range, intelligent decisions. This is both the grandeur and the terror of it. It is not limited to married people, of course. This longing for intimacy with another person dawns very early in youth with the change in body chemistry and remains relevant all through life, whether a person is married or not. The poets and the songwriters sometimes talk as if falling in love were the same thing as holiness. It is not. But since we are God's, we cannot understand ourselves apart from God. Human sexuality is deeply spiritual.

It has been recognized a long time that love has two directions. There is "need love," which we call eros. I love you because I need you. Then there is "gift-love," which we call agape. I love you purely unselfishly because you need me, but I have nothing to gain from you. Eros is born to all of us. Agape is not; it is God's pure grace. If we express any agape at all, it is the work of God in us. It is not natural. We have tended to call agape "good" and eros "bad," or at least tainted or selfish. This is an oversimplification. Eros is the longing of the soul for beauty and fulfillment. It is a gift of God to us. In our erotic love we are driven to God and to each other, and in these relationships our highest fulfillment is made possible. God himself addresses this need love of ours when he says, "Come to me, all who labor and are heavy laden, and I will give you rest" (Matt. 11:28). It is his valentine to us—"Be mine."

All good gifts from God have their dangerous side, and eros is no exception. The experience of love can be so all-consuming and so beautiful that we begin to think it to be the voice of God. After all, we have been taught that "God is love." But God is agape, gift-love. We look in the Scriptures and at the life of Jesus Christ to discover what we mean when we say, "God is love." Our mistake is when we look to our own eros, our own feelings of love, and call *that* God. When we make a god out of our own feelings and our own needs, we have created an idol; we worship a false god. God is love, but love is not God! God is agape, but the eros we experience is not God. It is a gift from God, but it is not to be identified as God.

It is no wonder we are fooled, because eros has such godlike qualities. Here is total commitment which rises above the self to serve the welfare of the beloved. Here is a creative power inspiring poetry, motivating hard work and great achievement. Here is such beauty that who could question its goodness and truth? How ready we are to give our unconditional obedience to eros! "Anything is right if it is for love," we fool ourselves into saying. Not only erotic love, but love for country or love for our friends or love for our family. It can all be demonic when we mistake it for the voice of God and let that "love" be our master.

A boy and a girl, each nineteen years of age, came to me to be married. They had known each other only one month and seemed unready to take such a step. They wanted to be married because they wanted to be married! They were swept up in eros for each other. I understood so well. Both of them came from broken homes. They felt they had found the answer to life in this great new emotion. I tried to get them to wait for one year, to court each other, to let their relationship deepen and be tested, but "love was God." They were mastered by eros and there was no persuading them. So, as I have done a number of times, I refused to perform the marriage. I could not take responsibility for the wedding. They were angry, and so was the girl's mother, who had already ordered the invitations. I had to say that I felt invitations were a very small thing compared to the lifetime of these two people. They were married by a judge, and after several rocky years the marriage broke up.

Eros is fickle. It is need love, and so our needs become

the authority. But our needs change. To be in love is to
intend and to promise lifelong faithfulness. Vows are made
all over the place with great sincerity. But eros promises
what it cannot produce. It is tied to the ups and downs of
our feelings and is dependent upon our human weakness.
We are sinners; we are not angels. When we make a selfless
promise, we cannot keep it for a week, let alone a lifetime.
We think that eros is the whole truth and that our great
motivation is going to last forever. But eros leaves and we
are let down. Suddenly the power and motive to fulfill our
grand promises is removed. Eros will let us down every
time, rising and falling like the tides. Love must be ruled by
God or it will become demonic.

When love is God, you change from a sexual being to a
sexual functionary. The Christian faith says you are a child
of God—you are not a function, you are a being. You are
important to God; you are an end in yourself, never to be
used as a means to someone else's end. If I mistake my love
for you as the voice of God, then I begin to use you to meet
my own love needs and I call it "right" for love's sake. You
become important to me not because you are a person but
because you serve a function. Your being disappears behind
your function. We make this separation of being and function all the time in the economic world. The worker is
valuable for his ability to produce and if he cannot fulfill that
function he is let go. The fact that he is a person has very
little to do with it. The customer is valuable to the salesman.
The salesman has plenty of smiles and attention to give as
long as a sale is possible, but when the function is over the
customer is quickly dropped. This dehumanizing experience has reached a crisis in our society. Nowhere is it more
devastating than in the area of sexuality. The *Playboy* philosophy is taken for granted on a wide scale. Sex is treated as

if it were merely a physiological function. Changing partners is as simple as trading old cars for new ones. There are
moral issues here. Keeping or breaking promises is a moral
issue. Justice or injustice is a moral issue. Charity or selfishness is a moral issue. The major issue, however, is that the
person is dehumanized and becomes a functionary. If I use
another person for my ecstasy, claiming that it is all right
because it is for love, I have in fact prostituted love and
sinned against man and God.

Mary of Magdala had been told many romantic things by
many Casanovas and she had whispered her own sincere
expressions of love. But she and her partners had existed to
benefit and stimulate and complement themselves. When
the function was over they could write each other off. There
is the great lie. No person can just be written off. When
Mary encountered Jesus she was confused. He loved her,
but he loved her for herself, not for something she could do
for him. His love did not depend on her performance. He
saw her as a person who had her own values. She could be
free in his presence. All the man-woman vibrations of eros
were there, but they were mastered by the Spirit of God—
by agape. All this power of love was directed to build her
up, not to tear her down. Mary was scared. She did not
know how to respond to this kind of love. The old way
would be to use her female attraction to control him, but his
unselfish love was deeply changing her. Her eros was being
mastered by agape, and the change in her life was overwhelming.

The real Valentine's Day question is, How do we master
love instead of being mastered by it? One of the most common ways to try to master love is to repress it. There is a
tradition in the church that chastity is virtuous and sensual
pleasure is evil. The apostle Paul seems to foster this belief.

Paul apparently had no time for marriage, although he did understand eros as a gift from God which can unite persons in a spiritual bond. (See how he compared life in Christ with marriage, and the church with a unified body of human beings who need each other.) Paul did take responsibility for his own opinions. When dealing with this subject, Paul never once said this was the word of God speaking. He always said it was his own opinion (I Cor. 7:6, 7, 12, 25, 40). All Paul could see was the end of the world at hand. There was so much territory to cover with the gospel that domestic concerns would only be a distraction taking time from the urgency of those last days. However, the end didn't come in his lifetime or in the lifetime of those who followed until now.

History has proved again and again that to repress eros only makes it more nagging and dominant. E. Stanley Jones tells of coming upon a hermit meditating in India. The first thing the hermit told him was that he had not looked upon the face of a woman for forty years. It was the first thing he said. For forty years he had been running away from sex, but it was the first thing he thought of. It is God's plan, not that you repress the gift he gives you, but that you master it and channel it in creative ways.

The key to this plan is the surrender of your love to Jesus Christ. The Holy Spirit then has the opportunity to come in and to master love at its source. The Holy Spirit does not deal in repression. The Holy Spirit does not simply pump up our willpower to control our desires by sheer grit. Rather, the Holy Spirit masters and directs our sexuality at its deepest subconscious levels. We find the power of our love directed to the person, not to his or her function. Like Jesus, now we are able to love those who serve no function for us at all. The people whom the world feels are not worth

loving we love by the inspiration of the Holy Spirit. This
frees us so wonderfully to enjoy and to relate to each other
without the threat of exploitation, without always trying to
second-guess the other person or wonder what his motives
may be. For example, we do not hide the fact that we enjoy
being men and women in each other's company. We are
aware of all the feminine and masculine vibrations, and yet
we can be comfortable and open; we can hug each other and
flirt and joke, for we are friends in Jesus Christ. The pseudo
seductiveness and permissiveness which the world knows so
well is not here to spoil the relationship where Jesus dwells.
Men and women can be real and can still be friends in
Christ.

Men and women traveled and camped together freely in
our Lord's company of disciples. He lived at the home of
Mary and Martha whenever he was in Bethany. There were
prostitutes who were converted and part of his company,
but scandal is something you cannot find. The enemies of
Jesus would have loved a juicy piece of scandal. They
searched for any reason at all by which they could discredit
him in public. Yet there is not one word of scandal in the
charges brought against him. You see, Christ is the purify-
ing force. When the Pharisees touched a leper, the Pharisees were made unclean. When Jesus Christ touched a leper,
the leper was made clean. And when Jesus Christ touches
your love, your eros, it is made clean.

Your value in my eyes is not that I need you but that
Christ died for you. This is our Christian way of saying God
loves you so much that he sent his only Son. This is our
Christian way of saying that you may very well perform a
function I need, you may be desirable to me, but my life has
been touched by the Spirit of Christ and so I see you
through different eyes. I see you as a being who belongs to

God and what I do to you I do to God! That changes everything! Paul expresses your value in this way: "Do you not know that your body is a temple of the Holy Spirit within you, which you have from God? You are not your own; you were bought with a price. So glorify God in your body" (I Cor. 6:19–20).

When you see a person being exploited, doesn't it cause your Christian heart to wrench? The Holy Spirit directing your love sends you out to do everything you can to rescue that person. The great social compassion of Christians is this Christ-directed eros caring about people who are being used by other people. We love "the least of these" to whom Christ referred. It is not a sterile, dutiful sort of love. It is the passion of our human hearts. In an age obsessed with sex we discover a new obsession, the Holy Spirit. He absorbs our human obsessions and directs them so beautifully for the good of everyone.

There is a mystery about this way of life which makes it the ultimate adventure. I wonder at myself as the passion I feel for my wife—wanting, needing, longing—is somehow changed into a desire to serve and to please her. I put aside my own selfish needs for the new and burning desire to meet her needs. How compelling is the racing of my blood in the presence of some stranger's need, the heartbreak of one who comes for counsel, the pleading eyes of someone encountered in a hospital. I marvel that I do not take advantage of them for my own needs, but long to enter theirs. It is courageous loving to allow the love of God to use and bless our eros; it is life's highest art. What an adventure, to put our instincts under the control of heaven and pour our life out for those closest to us. Without that, history loses its purpose and our meaning adds up to nothing.

Chapter 5

Two Major Problems

Five-year-old Steven and his younger sister were looking out through a hotel window at the end of a long hall. A woman stopped to talk with them. She knew that the parents of these youngsters had moved to this town because of their father's job but that due to the housing shortage they had been forced to live in the hotel for the time being. She said, "Steven, I'm sorry you don't have a home." They looked so forlorn standing there at the end of that bare hallway. But the youngster turned and replied quickly, "Oh, we have a home, we just don't have a house to put it in."

There is something refreshing about that point of view in a day when one out of three marriages ends in failure, when illegitimacy has tripled in the last twenty years, as has juvenile delinquency. The annual admissions to our mental hospitals is over two hundred thousand patients; 42 percent of the women with children under the age of eighteen work outside the home; 7.5 percent of the husbands hold two jobs. No wonder some experts are saying that the breakdown of the family is America's number one social problem.

Whether it is any comfort or not, it is worth noting that things were about the same in Abraham's day. There is an account in Gen. 16:1–16 which goes as far back on the other side of Jesus Christ as we are on this side, and the problems don't seem to have changed very much. Abraham and Sarah were great people of God, but they had a rough time keeping their marriage on the upward trail. The passage gives us a personal look at the intimate joys and storms of a family, with all the tangled emotions we recognize as our own.

The first problem that shakes up families now as then is *the unsurrendered ego.* Sarah and Abraham had not been able to have children and Sarah knew he was anxious about this. A male child was necessary to carry on the family, and in their day ancestors and heirs were of supreme importance. A person's identity, his whole meaning in life, revolved around the tribe and its perpetuation. But Sarah was barren. She felt bad enough disappointing her husband, but this also meant that her own longing for motherhood was unfulfilled. She had failed; Abraham had failed; neither of their egos was free to fail. Sarah was afraid that Abraham would not love her just for what she was, so she insisted he become the father of a child by Hagar, her handsome Egyptian maid. This was sometimes done in that culture without any eyebrows being lifted. So the world sees Abraham take another wife, but the world does not see into the soul of his marriage to Sarah, where two egos are battling it out in a life-or-death struggle.

This battle rages on in many marriages. Most people come into marriage with a preconceived vision of their ideal partner. For the wife it may be the improbable balance of virility, suaveness, and intellectual depth. The husband's vision of his ideal wife combines sex-kitten, businesswoman, and homemaker. One day, well into the marriage, these two suddenly see the truth and realize they don't know each other at all. One woman said, "My husband seems like a mysterious island that I am always encircling without ever finding a place to land." (Paul Tournier, *Escape from Loneliness,* p. 32; The Westminster Press, 1962.)

In premarital counseling we hope to help the couple become realistic enough to see the difference between the vision and the facts. Too often when they do recognize this with the head, the heart passes it off, pretending the partner will fit the image later on. So the marriage begins with the battle lines already drawn: two egos, two gods, each insisting on his or her own definition of the marriage relationship. If you've ever wondered why so many marriages seem bland or dull it is because this battle of the wills has been resolved into a peaceful coexistence. Of course there are times of happiness and love, but basically it is a "stalemate." There is no growth at the heart of the relationship, only a deadlock.

The good news is that faith in Jesus Christ can change the soul of the marriage from a battleground to a meeting ground. He enables two people to come together from the struggles of the world and feel safe, accepted, and loved. When they each give him their egos, he purifies them and gives them back. This is not an easy process, of course, because it means the death of the old self and all those precious preconceptions. But when we discover Jesus' acceptance of us even in our failures, when we experience his love for us, then our levels of selfishness, jealousy, and pride can afford to lower. We are released from the prison of our egos. No longer do we have to make everybody fit our idea of what is right. We can accept others as they are, not as we think they should be. This acceptance begins with our own spouse.

What a beautiful discovery that I can love you whether or not you come up to my expectations! I don't have to change you. If you need changing, God will do that. When we carry this freedom into marriage we no longer have to prove anything to each other except our love. It is great to be able to be a child with my wife. It is wonderful not to have to prove to her that I am a man. She knows that I am and affirms it; I know it and affirm it. But I really am a child so often, and now I can accept that because she does. At other times, she can count on me to be strong and to allow her to be the child, when that's how she feels. At still other times, we can both be children in the soul of our marriage.

Selfish people can accept selfish people and love them deeply without always trying to change them, because they themselves are loved by Jesus Christ. Then the miracle: we do change, drawn upward by the challenge of that kind of love.

One young husband was a carpenter, proud of the cabinets he had built. He kept his yard neat for the neighborhood to admire. Anything to do with housekeeping, however, was totally outside his realm. His father had never helped in the house and he was convinced that his manhood was at stake every time the subject came up. The conflict surfaced within the first few months of the marriage because her father had always helped in the home, especially with the dishes. She had seen her parents have some of their happiest conversations doing dishes together. "No way!" exclaimed her groom. "That's woman's work!" And with that he left her alone at the sink and buried himself in the evening paper. The years passed and the hour after supper each night was a full-blown barrier between them. Everytime they sidestepped it, the barrier grew.

Then in a life-changing week he gave his life to Christ. Many things immediately began to happen, including his desire to express the overflowing love of God to his wife. Suddenly, there it was: the finished supper with its dirty dishes. He groaned deeply within. The whole matter had become such an issue that surely he could start somewhere else! This was too painful! But no. It had to be the dishes because that was where his pride was greatest. He got up from the table, cleared the dishes to the sink, and proceeded to prepare the dishwater before his stunned wife could ask what this was all about. It was the beginning of a whole new leap forward in their love. They let down the barriers, stopped defending their resentments, and experienced the love of Jesus in the intimate relationship of their home.

An unsurrendered ego is the first problem in preventing the Christian home.

The second major problem in a marriage is often *an ignorance about sex.* Sarah had this sense of failure with her husband, so half trying to please him and half trying to get him to quit nagging, she needled him into a sexual relationship with another woman. Abraham went along with the game. It was quite legal and proper in those days. The trouble is that it backfired, as sexual relationships outside of marriage usually do. The thing did not accomplish what either of them had hoped. It only drove them further apart and almost wrecked Abraham's faith in God.

Let us hope that young people now preparing for marriage will be more intelligent about training their children in the meaning of sex than most of their parents have been. This subject will never be fully taught in the schools. We cannot deal fully with sex apart from God or apart from deep love-relationships, and we can't have either in the classroom! Ignorance about sex can only be fully dealt with in the home, and maybe in the church. We have to realize, in the first place, that all communication between people is sexual. There is an intimacy of one degree or another every time two human beings touch, look into each other's eyes, or share their feelings with each other. This is good, this is godly, this is not something from which to run away. There is a mystery here: heart reaching out to heart, which finds its pinnacle of joy in the actual sexual relationships of husband and wife. This mystery is not one that we ought to fear.

In the Scriptural account of the Creation we find God creating male and female, bringing them together in sexual union and calling it good! This is holy ground—two bodies united, two spirits mingling in an ecstasy that transcends earth. Here the man knows what it means to be a man and the woman what it means to be a woman! Each finds identity in relationship to the other. The thing that Abraham and Sarah discovered, as have a large percentage of men and women since Eden, is that sexual intercourse is a lie outside of marriage, outside of the union of two persons in a lifetime commitment to each other. Both Abraham and Sarah thought it was a pretty neat arrangement. But before they were through Sarah was enraged with jealousy, blaming it all on her husband; Abraham had checked out and wasn't communicating with anybody. Hagar and her child were deeply injured, and even the descendants of the homeless Ishmael were marked by the experience.

I don't know why we stay so ignorant about sex except that we want to be! The open discussion about sex today doesn't bother me much, except when it says that sex is harmless outside of marriage. That's where the lie needs to be exposed. Hardly a week goes by that I don't talk with someone whose psychological and emotional life is all scrambled up over some sexual relationship outside of marriage. Before, during, after marriage, it's all the same! If it's outside, it's trouble! God intended this relationship to be such a deep revelation of one soul to another that unless two people take full responsibility for each other the act is a profoundly dishonest experience. Do they share the same hope and destiny? Do they each commit themselves to the

other's future? Do they pledge their faith to each other
"from this day forward, for better, for worse, for richer, for
poorer, in sickness and in health, to love and to cherish, till
death us do part"? If they do, then it is a mountaintop of
truth and beauty!

Not only does a lack of appreciation for the profound
meaning of sex upset a marriage, but so does an ignorance
of its psychological and physiological meanings. A great
many married men have never understood the saying of
Balzac that "a woman is like a musical instrument, and he
that would draw forth harmony must learn how to play." It's
a sin the way some husbands are so ignorant that they never
learn to satisfy and fulfill the needs of their wives. God is
concerned about this, I can assure you. There are all too
many marriages that have never experienced physical harmony because the husband is a blunderer. He does not
know and will not learn to woo his wife and gently lead her
to his own peak of physical response. When the two learn
this art of physical harmony they discover a new degree of
spiritual harmony as well. This is God's will for them both.
This kind of interaction and personal development can take
place only in a permanent union where two persons over the
years know each other and discover together the fulfillment
of themselves. It requires time and intimacy and opportunity for companionship, and a continuous embroidering
upon this creative expression between a man and a woman
which neither of them can carry out alone. In our days and
nights of rushing and pressure and moneymaking, it is not
easy to find time for this. A married couple needs to discipline themselves to put some of the other responsibilities
aside and take time just to be together. This is God's will
for your fulfillment.

This has been a word especially to Abraham. Let me say

a word to Sarah. God has a beautiful way of making sure that little children are looked after. Much of a woman's sexual energy and desire is diverted to the care of her children. The dependence of the child before birth, the nursing and early years, even on through adolescence and youth the young wife is using up her energies on her children. Often she does not hunger for the biological union as she once did, and should later on. At the same time the husband is out achieving in his vocation and laboring in the world. For all his achievements and salary and honors, life has its real meaning in personal relationships. Mother has a deep relationship with her children, but nowhere else, and with no one else, can the husband have total intimacy of personal involvement except with his wife. She alone can fulfill the deepest meaning in life for him. You see, in God's plan sexual intercourse is not only a matter of physical satisfaction, but a matter of spiritual necessity. A man becomes starved for the mystery of the one-flesh union, which the New Testament calls as profound a mystery as Christ's relationship to his church. As the Bible puts it, "to know" his wife! When through ignorance or weariness a man's wife deprives him of this intimacy, this total involvement which only she can fulfill, she is asking him for more than patience. She is depriving his life of meaning in a most highly spiritual sense. How often we who work with people see this crippling sense of frustration turn a husband's love into a secret hate. At this very point some men, through ignorance or weakness or sheer starvation, enter into emotional and physical relationships outside of marriage.

We need a lot more frankness and understanding about these things. The problems are not merely physical, they are spiritual. Where needs are not satisfied, a spiritual separation sets in which ends up in a polite tolerance of one another if not open hostility. It is God's plan that marriage and family living should be more than polite tolerance or open hostility. It should be the "splice of life"! But into all homes there comes trouble, because we are human and we are born to trouble. For every home and every marriage there is redemption in turning to Jesus Christ.

We don't change people. We love them as they are with the love of Jesus Christ. Then as God works in us the other person decides to change! There is no beauty to compare with loving and accepting each other in the midst of the problems and letting Christ's love do the changing in his own good time. When God's will becomes personally important to both parties in a Christian marriage then, only then, is a Christian home possible. Then the soul of the marriage is not what the husband thinks it ought to be, not what the wife or children think it ought to be. Together they begin to find out what Christ's vision of their marriage is and what Christ wants their home to be.

Chapter 6

Two More Major Problems

An angry father asked his teen-age son, "Where did you go?" The boy was trying to sneak into the house late at night. His answer was, "Nowhere!" The father snapped back: "Oh, grow up. Stop hanging around the public square and wandering up and down the street. Go to school. Night and day you torture me. Night and day you waste your time having fun!"

That familiar dialogue was translated by Samuel Kramer from a four-thousand-year-old Sumerian tablet. Thus, some of the problems of living together as a family have not changed much since ancient times.

Sometimes we tend to think that our times are different, and in a sense they are. Human knowledge doubles every ten years or less. With the world shrinking to the size of a village, different cultures are being thrown together. But basically human problems are the same as they have always been.

An intimate look at the family life of ancient Abraham and Sarah in Gen., ch. 16, makes this truth very clear. There were four major problems in that home which created spiritual tensions and conflicts similar to those we often have in our homes today. In the last chapter I dealt with the problems of the unsurrendered ego and ignorance about sex. Now I want to explore the other two problems which are making the family so hard to maintain.

First, the *weakness of the husband in the family.* Abraham
and Sarah had gotten into a bad situation at home. Sarah felt
that she had failed her husband by not bearing him children,
and Abraham had failed to make Sarah feel loved and accepted for herself in spite of her barrenness. They agreed
that Abraham would have a child by his wife's Egyptian
maid, Hagar. Then the whole affair backfired. The maid and
Sarah flamed into mutual hostilities. When she tried to talk
to Abraham about it he washed his hands of the whole
thing. Stepping away from any responsibility, he simply
said: "Sarah, she's your maid. You do with her whatever
you want to." After that, things became so bad that Hagar
ran away and got lost in the desert. Here is a father and
husband abdicating his responsibilities in the home, dump-
ing it all in his wife's lap. The consequences are frightening.

A profound disturbance has come into the family in our
time. It all began when our urban, technical civilization took
the husband and father out of the home. For the first time,
the father's place of work is far removed from his living
place. The physical presence of the father is gone, and the
mother has had to take over many of his traditional responsibilities. We hear a lot today about "identity crisis." Many
children do not know who they are because they feel rejected by the father. They simply can't see him; they cannot
identify with him. Girls grow up insecure about marriage
because they have no strong male figure to relate to in those
formative years. Boys grow up confused about what it
means to be a man because there is no model in the home.
When dad does come home, he's too tired for any creative
conflict. He abdicates his role as father and tries to be a pal
to his son. You don't have to have conflict with "pals." But
boys can find plenty of pals. They have only one who can
be "father"!

Not long ago, I was talking with a group of youth. One of the boys was moaning about having to get a haircut. His hair was very thick and long and his father had contended with him for some time about it. Finally he laid down the ultimatum: either get a haircut by Mother's Day or leave home! After the young man had made a federal case out of this in our conversation, one of the other boys who was present told how he didn't have any father in his home to give orders. Then, looking at the lad with the long hair, he said, "I wish I had your problem!" How great is the need for the father image in the home!

About the same time that most fathers stopped working where they lived, women developed a strong drive for independence. After all, what wife wants to be a prisoner on a plot of ground 50 by 100 feet while her husband is out seeing the world? One young woman got a university degree and went to work. Now she could leave her parents and call her own tune. She was able to become independent financially, intellectually, and morally. When she met the man of her dreams she never thought about giving up all of the things that her independent income provided: the fine clothes, travel, sports, freedom. She just wanted the bliss of marriage. However, her groom wants her to quit working because he doesn't earn much more than she does and it's humiliating to him. His role as provider is threatened. Some take exception to this, but the preponderance of studies conclude that by nature the male is the aggressor and better equipped to be the provider. It is at least foolish to deny that the male is more muscular and the female more passive. Inevitably the task of childbearing and intimate child-raising is given to the female. This itself determines her role as distinct from the male. The extent to which these innate physical and psychological characteristics have determined social rules is immense. To the degree that roles are socially conditioned, they are changeable. However, even social conditioning is so deeply ingrained that direct and immediate efforts to change it are potentially disastrous.

The man feels his responsibility is being cut away by the wife's independence. He feels more like a boarder than a partner in the tasks of family and home, so he begins to withdraw. He is less and less ready to assert himself with the children. He plows his frustrations back into his work. Perhaps he works more overtime or takes on two or three jobs. He's in competition with his wife. Maybe he can earn enough so that she will respect him and he can do the nice things for her that his heart longs to do. Then at an early age his heart burns out and the dilemma is solved by death, at least for him.

Ask counselors and medical doctors what is happening today! This equalization of men and women is creating an emotional and moral turmoil and producing a nation of neurotics. Men and women were created to need and fulfill each other, not to be independent of each other. Paul Tournier, world-famous psychologist, puts it flatly when he says: "Nature has willed love to be aggressive in the man and passive in the woman. No one can change that. Love in the man needs to conquer. . . . In the woman's soul there is something that impels her to refuse that which she desires: she says no to the man all the while seeking to be conquered in spite of her refusal." (*Escape from Loneliness,* p. 72.) Tournier goes on to point out that the woman's coyness usually increases the man's desire to conquer. Too often today the man never has the challenge. The woman has insisted on becoming like the man. No longer submissive, she is now the aggressor and the provider. Her daughters imitate her independence. They wear men's clothes, they hitchhike, they boldly pursue their boyfriends. The next step is the mental health clinic, so nervous and confused are they about conquering like men when deep in their souls they cry out to be conquered.

In the face of this confusion, men are becoming like women. The father gives up his role as conqueror. His sons become passive, style their clothes and their hair like girls, and decide on a vocation where they can be the most secure with the least amount of risk. There is conflict in the man between his masculine drive to conquer and this new role of being passive. I am overwhelmed in my counseling by the number of husbands who are so confused about their identity as men that they are no longer sure they love their wives. The protective, assertive role has been taken from him and he is confused.

Right after the husband leaves the counselor, the wife comes in another door and she says something like this: "I am disgusted with my husband. He's not a man, he's a child. He is so hesitating I have to make all the decisions. He plays with his hobbies and he leaves all the responsibilities to me. If only I had a husband I could lean on!" No wonder so many people have a fuzzy understanding about God the Father! The father in the home is fuzzy! Lack of trust in the earthly father leaves a person pretty confused about the heavenly Father.

The fourth major problem in the family is the *lack of love!* This begins because not every couple who comes to the altar to be married is brought there by God. Many are brought there by lust or by social ambition or convention. There are wolves who come disguised in bride's or groom's clothing, and many families get launched for the wrong reasons. Many people think that love is something you "fall into." They have no more idea about the sacrificial nature of love than the man in the moon. When the honeymoon wears off they discover it's an ugly thing that's left, these two trying to use each other for their own self-interests. Love is not something you feel, love is something you do! Love means helping someone else become what he or she is capable of becoming.

I don't know why it was in Abraham's home, but love was gone. Here was Hagar carrying Abraham's child and giving her life in service to Sarah. Yet Abraham washed his hands of her, and Sarah forced her out. No love there. In Gen. 16:7–9, we find that God loved her even if Mr. and Mrs. Abraham didn't. Hagar had run away. She was lost and exhausted in the wilderness, "and [the LORD] said, 'Hagar, maid of Sarai, where have you come from and where are you going?' She said, 'I am fleeing from my mistress Sarai.' The angel of the LORD said to her, 'Return to your mistress, and submit to her.' "

There are many today who are running away from home and its responsibilities, running away from the rejection they feel! Teen-agers, wives, husbands—running away from the hypocrisy, the dishonesty, and the unloveliness at home. But where are they going? What waits for them in the wilderness? Certainly not the solution to their problems. We carry our problems with us. The unwanted child of Hagar, Ishmael, became a juvenile delinquent and a criminal, "a wild ass of a man, his hand against every man and every man's against him; and he shall dwell over against all his kinsmen." So writes the author of Gen. 16:12. There's got to be a better way than that.

The Lord points Hagar to the only way that will really work: "Return to your mistress . . . ," and then that great word echoed later in the New Testament, "and submit to her!" For all its tests and all its tribulations, the family is still the only place where a person learns to love. We should include the larger family of the church, which is where so many learn to love. No other agency in our society fulfills the function of forming the loving, mature, flexible personalities that can deal with life in a creative way. Remember, we defined love as helping the other person become fulfilled. To "submit to each other in love" is the mutual act of fulfilling and being fulfilled. Love is not something that is taught; love is absorbed from life's earliest experiences. I suppose that the first thing parents owe to their children is to love each other openly and demonstratively! Homes where adults and children aren't afraid to love and be loved, where mothers enjoy being women and where fathers enjoy being men, become a spiritual dynamo of joy and service. Dorothy Nolte's poem "Children Learn What They Live" adds to this:

> If a child lives with criticism,
> He learns to condemn.
> If a child lives with hostility,
> He learns to fight.
> If a child lives with ridicule,
> He learns to be shy.
> If a child lives with shame,
> He learns to feel guilty.
> If a child lives with tolerance,
> He learns to be patient.
> If a child lives with encouragement,
> He learns confidence.
> If a child lives with praise,
> He learns to appreciate.
> If a child lives with fairness,
> He learns justice.

If a child lives with security,
  He learns to have faith.
If a child lives with approval,
  He learns to like himself.
If a child lives with acceptance and friendship,
  He learns to find love in the world.

I'm going to say something that is highly practical, and yet at first it will sound like a pious platitude. It is this: Jesus Christ holds the solution to the dilemma of the modern family. The Bible says that the relationship of husband and wife should be like the relationship of Christ to the church. The church is not a democracy nor a republic nor a dictatorship. It cannot be compared to any political structure. The church is a body; we compare it to a biological organism. Christ is the head of this body; he sends directives out to all its parts and they are subject to him. The parts obey because they have submitted, trusting him to protect and direct and care for them in the best way to fulfill their potential. It is just this way with the Christian home. Consider J. B. Phillips' translation of Eph. 5:21–31: " 'Fit in with' one another, because of your common reverence for Christ. You wives must learn to adapt yourselves to your husbands, as you submit yourselves to the Lord, for the husband is the 'head' of the wife in the same way that Christ is the head of the Church and savior of the body. The willing subjection of the Church to Christ should be reproduced in the submission of wives to their husbands. But, remember, this means that the husband must give his wife the same sort of love that Christ gave to the Church, when he sacrificed himself for her. . . . Men ought to give their wives the love they naturally have for their own bodies. The love a man gives his wife is the extending of his love for himself to enfold her. Nobody ever hates or neglects his own body; he feeds it and looks after it. And that is what Christ does for his body, the Church. And we are all members of that body. . . . 'For this cause shall a man leave his father and his mother, and shall cleave to his wife; and the twain shall become one flesh.' " (J. B. Phillips, *The New Testament in Modern English;* The Macmillan Company, 1958.)

Who finds it hard to submit to sacrificial love like that? You can have my life any day if you will love me like that! The Christian home is not a dictatorship where the father is a tyrant. The Christian home is not a democracy where every member is equal. The Christian home is not a republic where the parents have authority only by consent of the children. The Christian home is an organic unity like a human body. It is based on mutual subordination, every member bound to the others in a mutual love and trust. The father is "the head." The wife and children work in harmony with him like "arms and organs" because they believe in him. They know that everything he does is meant for their best interests and that he will sacrifice everything for them to care for them and to help them grow to their fullest potential, even as Christ "emptied himself, taking the form of a servant" (Phil. 2:7). It's a great experience learning how to love like this as a family. The thing that counts in the Christian home is not how much you talk about your faith and how pious you are, but whether you are fun to live with! Does the joy of Jesus Christ radiate in the midst of that family circle day after day? Are we free to be vulnerable to each other's demands, or are we still trying to manipulate one another to get what we want? Christ's kind of love never fails.

One father was so deeply involved in the church and scouting activities that he was completely out of touch with his daughter. When he realized this he dropped some of his activities, worthwhile as they were, and spent more time at home with his daughter. Lo and behold, his efforts got no results. Then God revealed a great thing to him. His daughter did not need more of his time; she only needed to have all of him in the brief times they had. He discovered that when he was reading or playing games or doing things with her his mind was always on something else. He was also talking with his wife or watching television. His daughter never had more than half of him. She felt rejected and unloved because of this. All of us do. Christ's kind of love is undivided attention. This father discovered that he did not have to entertain his family. All he had to do was tune in to them, be present with them as Christ is present with each of us, taking each one seriously as a person. Oh the beauty of really listening and really watching as a loved one tries to tell you something!

I have discovered a painful thing in my life. If I sit with my finger in the newspaper and indulgently watch my wife or daughter as she tries to tell me something, I am really saying: "O.K., we've got a three-minute limit on this conversation. The paper is more important than you!" To "submit to one another out of reverence for Christ" means a constant growth process for every member of the family. Even parents can be human and vulnerable. They need not think that because they are parents they have to be prophets and teachers and always right. To admit our mistakes, to expose our weaknesses, to cast down our pride is a very Christlike exercise in the family.

There is such beauty in discovering Christ in our family circles as we submit to one another in love. Why miss it one more day?

Chapter 7

The Covenants in Marriage

A husband and wife were driving in the country and reminiscing about their earlier years. The wife said, "Do you remember our first car and how close we used to sit?" With a twinkle in his eye her husband answered, "I haven't moved."

In almost half of the marriages in America the move is farther apart than a car seat. Our divorce rate is now the highest in the world. The American way seems to let people into marriage for the price of a license but let them out of marriage only at the emotional cost of a heart transplant. In Russia, interestingly, they have an eight-week waiting period from the time the couple applies for the license until the wedding. It eliminates a lot of marriages for the wrong reasons. There are some counselors in America who are recommending a premarital contract. (Norman Sheresky and Marya Mannes, "A Radical Guide to Wedlock," *Saturday Review,* July 29, 1972, p. 33.) Potential marriage partners explore and actually put into writing their motives for marrying; their intentions for children, for economic responsibility, for property sharing; and future alimony should the marriage fail. In the church we insist on some form of premarital counseling and a personal relationship between the couple and the pastor. Statistics reveal that couples married in the church have a 50 percent better chance of staying together than couples married outside the church. What is there about the Christian approach to marriage that is different?

The Christian faith holds that a personal relationship of love with God is the supreme value in life. This relationship with God is inseparable from our understanding of ourselves and our relationship to each other. The deeper we experience love, the more profoundly we experience God. The deepest and most profound human relationship is the experience between one man and one woman who come together in a lifelong marriage. This is expressed in Scripture by passages like Gen. 2:24: "Therefore a man leaves his father and his mother and cleaves to his wife, and they become one flesh." In Eph., ch. 5, mutual self-giving is discussed, comparing marriage to the relationship between Christ and the church. Bride and groom give their lives each to the other in an enlightened self-sacrifice. Since both are one flesh, to cherish and nourish the other is to love yourself. This kind of relationship has to be cultivated. The powerful romantic forces which drove them together in the beginning lose their urgency. The overwhelming obligations of society and children and home soon threaten to squeeze out the growing relationship of the husband and the wife.

Tragically, some young people believe that marriage will suddenly transform two lonely people into full-blown perfect oneness and security. This one-flesh union is a process, a state which is built slowly over the years. Let this be a warning to young people who slip carelessly into marriage hoping to solve all their problems; or to those who, guided mostly by their passions, are not prepared to sacrifice their lives for one another. Let this be a warning to married people who are tempted to run away from their marriages because they are too selfish to work at building them right!

Let this be a warning to those who insist on divorce, that they must also be prepared to endure the hurt that results in cutting themselves off from the order of creation.

Why are we, husband and wife, the only ones for each other? Not because of fate, not because it's in the stars, but because marriage means that we have become part of each other. We are no longer alone. The two are becoming one in a relationship that is total and unique. When my partner in marriage becomes cold and empty I must face the fact that I have caused this. She is never what she is apart from me once God has given us each other. Not only is she bone of my bones, but she is boredom of my boredom, and loneliness of my loneliness, and love of my love, and joy of my joy!

If this relationship is to grow into the joyful union God intends it to be, there is work to be done. The task begins in some mutual agreements. Let's call them "covenants," since each partner of a covenant is still bound to it even when the other does not fulfill the agreement. That's how God relates to us, and in Christ's love we relate to each other. If I fail you, and you continue to reach out to me in our covenant, the wall between us can't grow much thicker. Sooner or later I melt and take up the covenant again myself.

The covenant of time is one. There is no substitute for time with each other. Yet this is the first thing to go as men and women become engrossed in climbing the ladder of success. People can become married to their businesses, their lodges, their do-gooding, their politics, or even to their church organizations. I cannot be married to these things and to my wife at the same time and expect the relationship to go anywhere that is meaningful, any more than I can be committed to two or more wives at the same time and expect any one of the relationships to mature. Perhaps we can commit adultery in more ways than one, being unfaithful to each other in favor of those other things.

The covenant of time also requires that we watch out for the children. How quickly they can come between us! Add up the chauffering, the doctor and dentist appointments, the Little League, the Indian Guides, the P.T.A., the lessons, the lodges, and the costs for all of these things which increase financial anxiety. I suspect that one reason our children take so long to find themselves and why many of them drift into other life-styles is that we have not allowed them to be children. We push our kids for academics and music and athletics and hobbies and clubs until they have no time to dream, no years to be carefree, no months just to develop a sensitivity to nature and to one another. All this pressure we put upon our children also takes its toll on adults. Soon the role of husband and wife, which no one else can fulfill, is replaced by the role of father and breadwinner, the role of mother and housekeeper. Someone said, "Put the first baby second." It is a fact that the best gift we can give our children is for mother and dad to still be friends. If we fail in this, we have failed to teach our children the best lesson, and when they are gone we will not only have lost them, we will have lost each other.

Time together has two dimensions—quantity and quality. It takes a lifetime to discover what love is. Marriage is not the result of love; it is the opportunity for love. It is not destiny that makes your partner your one true love. It is life! It is the hardships that we have faced together, it is bending over the children's sickbeds, it is struggling with budgets, it is the million smiles and the thousand hours in each other's arms. It is the vacations together and the conversations by the fire. It is the growing reverence for each other which comes only with the passing of time. One of the great privileges of being a pastor is that it sends me on the run to spend time with my wife. As I share the anticipation of a young couple planning marriage, the agony of a breaking home, the loneliness and the pain of one whose partner has died, I can hardly wait to be with my own dearest one and spend that precious time together which so quickly slips past us.

It is important *how* we spend that time together. A young wife asked a jeweler how she could preserve her wedding ring and he answered, "By soaking it in dishwater three times a day." I notice that most weddings these days are double ring ceremonies. Even with dishwashers there is rinsing and cleaning up that can be done together. There is a quality of caring for each other which takes place in the daily chores of life. It was a long time before I learned that my newspaper was a wall that separated me from my wife. Earlier I mentioned that when I indulgently put my finger in the page and lowered the paper temporarily as she was trying to communicate with me, I was really saying to her: "You are worth just three minutes of my time. Hurry up!" It is so easy for us husbands to withdraw into ourselves. The world has been on our backs all day and we want to escape into our reading or the television. We just aren't up to solving domestic problems on top of a busy day. Sometimes we feel that our wives can't understand our professional and political interests. We may be fascinating conversationalists with our friends and say little to our wives at home. A wife needs a husband to talk to her, and the fact that he is talking is far more important than the content of what he says. She needs to feel needed by him, to know that she is important enough for him to share with her. She needs him to lean on her for advice and counsel and encouragement. On the other hand, the wife needs to realize that her husband is interested in ideas and that if she is not enthusiastic about his ideas, there is little point in his exposing them. Her husband is not looking for technical competence in his wife. He has that in his colleagues and his associates. What he needs is for her to show an interest in his life just as she needs him to show an interest in her day at home with the children. The center of his life is his professional activity. Many men live in a perpetual conflict between their home and their work. The tension weighs down on their whole effectiveness. Caught between the demands of their wives and their businesses, they don't know how to allot their time. Feeling that they are misunderstood, they withdraw into themselves.

How beautiful the quality of life together can be when husband and wife make a covenant of time! They might agree to spend fifteen minutes a day sharing in depth, discussing neither children nor work nor friends but rather what is going on inside of each other at a feeling level. Then they might spend at least an hour a day, at night perhaps, after everything is quiet, facing each other eye-to-eye and going over the events of the day. They need each other's encouragement. They need to be interested in everything that interests the other. They need to develop an emotional and intellectual companionship. They need to share their intuitions and take time to explore each other's problems or to meditate in each other's presence.

Table-talk has always been a great festival time in our family. After that the children ask to be excused, which we were glad to grant. Those next moments alone together over coffee in relaxed conversation have been some of the great building blocks of our marriage. Many couples have discovered the importance of going out to dinner alone once a week. One fellow attributed his happy fifty years of marriage to the fact that he and his wife went out to dinner twice a week. She went out on Mondays and Wednesdays and he went out on Tuesdays and Thursdays. There are some couples who have discovered the importance of going out *once* a week *together.* Not dining necessarily, but looking across the table at each other over a hamburger with no interruptions, and getting caught up. One counselor made a discovery that enabled many disintegrating marriages to get back together. He suggested that once a month each mate write the other a thoughtful love letter. Perhaps no other covenant between husband and wife is more important than the covenant of time.

One other covenant which suggests the idea I am trying to communicate is the covenant of honesty. Paul Tournier tells of a patient who was hesitant to tell his wife the things he shared with his counselor. He wanted to take the step to be liberated from this burden, but could he risk upsetting his wife? The counselor could not advise him what to do. It was a personal decision which must be made by weighing all sorts of factors of which the counselor knew nothing. In order to encourage him to make the decision, Tournier began to relate how he was able to share everything with his wife. As he talked about the importance of complete, mutual openness between husband and wife, he suddenly remembered something that he had kept from her. It was something that would be easier to share than the matter that was troubling his patient. Several times Tournier had promised himself that he would tell her, but each time he postponed the confession. Now he must do it; he would not be able to see this patient again until he had put everything right with his own wife. (Paul Tournier, *The Adventure of Living,* p. 67; Harper & Row, Publishers, Inc., 1965.)

Some years ago in a magazine interview, Erich Fromm said a provocative thing: "There are no statistics, but I think most so-called good marriages, those that avoid the divorce courts, are marriages in which two people have found a common interest, don't dislike each other, are decent to each other, and have a common interest in their children, but no very intense or deep feeling." (*McCall's,* quoted in "Quote," Jan. 2, 1966.) How many marriages become that "blah" sort of humdrum because husband and wife have never launched the adventure of honesty? Here are two people who live under the same roof, whose bodies become one but whose souls are miles apart; strangers after twenty years because they hide a little here and a little there or lie to each other. The marriage slowly sinks into the gloomy twilight, a mere routine of living together, and finally sets in utter boredom.

A grumpy uncle was berating his nephew about the younger generation and how easy life is for them. "You fellows expect too much," he said. "Why, do you know what I was getting when I married your Aunt Sarah?" "No," replied the nephew, "and I'll bet you didn't either." I guess none of us really knows what we are getting when we first enter into marriage. The wonderful adventure is in growing, learning to be transparent, willing to risk the pain and conflict of complete openness in order to find real fulfillment. We so quickly lose the spirit of adventure. Soon we lie to ourselves, we live in a delusion, and fossilize. Only in the encounter with another person can we learn to know ourselves. I suppose that happens occasionally in a small group or in the counselor's office or in the company of dear friends, but in marriage we have a lifelong arena for the constant renewal of this adventure in living. Slowly we come out from behind the curtain and explore the infinite facets of each other. A lifetime together is a frightening and awesome thing—to share every strength and every weakness, to enjoy every success and to bear together every sorrow, to suffer every defeat, to gaze upon that same face each morning; to live with the lift of laughter and the cry of despair, to experience the tension of lips and then the softness of them. We are not the same as we were yesterday. We are changing up or down for good or ill, and the covenant of transparency must be kept daily. The apostle Paul said, "Do not let the sun go down on your anger" (Eph. 4:26). Some days you may not have the strength to dump it all before the sun goes down, but don't wait past the second day. One couple has an agreement that if there is something between them and it cannot surface within forty-eight hours they ask for an extension. It will be shared. The covenant of transparency is kept, for in the meantime they have admitted that there is a problem.

Distrust does to a marriage what termites do to a wooden building. I have known men who bottled up so much inside because they were too weak to encounter their wives or because their wives were not skillful enough to draw them out. Every time a man hides a little more he tightens the band around his heart. When it snaps, his wife is a widow. Behind the word of God "It is not good that the man should be alone" (Gen. 2:18) is the human need to be totally known by another person and accepted in that knowledge as we really are. There can be no real peace in any of us until what is deep inside has surfaced and been shared with another person. Only God knows us as we really are, and he is one with whom we can share in the ultimate way. However, the presence of God must be meditated. Who in all the world can really know me, warts and all, naked in body, mind, motives, and feelings? Who but my spouse? There in that mutual transparency we find God, his love, his acceptance, and our own fulfillment.

It is not easy, nor is it child's play, but there is a Way back to Eden for those who are lost. That way is Jesus Christ, who knows your heartaches and who comes to you in your loneliness to lead you on the road of healing. To the homosexual he gives the power to change. To the adulterer he gives forgiveness and the way out of the forest. To the divorced person he gives the call to a new beginning. To the spinster he gives new avenues to love and serve others. To the married he gives the courage and the inspiration to build a heaven on earth. The Way of Christ is the way of sacrificial love, serving and giving the self to the other! It involves trust and honesty. That is part and parcel of New Testament salvation! Marriage becomes the primary arena where our salvation is worked out. If Christ is not saving us in our marriage, then it is time for a deep searching of souls and long talks with each other. It takes work to build a marriage, and Christ will help you, but you've got to invite him in.

We were having a spiritual-life mission in our church. A married couple who were counselors to the young people had planned to be there to back up the youth. It was the opening night and only the husband showed up. On the second night, the wife was not there again. On the third day she met with her Women's Society circle and the speaker of the preaching mission was the leader. The message was just for her. In fact, it got so close to her aching heart that she got up and left the meeting crying to her hostess, "I can't take any more of this." The next night she attended the worship service and the theme was on God in marriage. Both husband and wife dared to face themselves during that hour. At the close of the service she was down at the altar in prayer, hand in hand with her husband. The final night of the mission they went down together again for prayer. The next day they stopped by my office. The husband said: "You didn't know it, but last week before this preaching mission started, I had rented an apartment and we were planning to get a divorce! Now it's all right—everything is right in Christ!" That is because in Him trust and transparency is restored.

There are other covenants of marriage. Each couple can explore the options together, but time and honesty are where it all begins and continues.

PART THREE

Then There Were More (The Children)

Chapter 8

My First Christmas as a Grandfather

Christmas meant something new to me the year I first became a grandfather. Shortly after Thanksgiving I began to realize that the carols had a new dimension to them and my eyes were quicker to fill with tears when we sang. I asked myself why this was, and the answer came quickly. A baby had been born to our family, our first grandchild. For years the wonder of Christmas had come to me in high-sounding theological expressions of how God was at work in Jesus. Of course, that is important all year long, but Christmas has suddenly become much more simple. Its magic is the mystery of a new baby. In fact, God confronts us in every new baby.

All babies are replicas of "The Baby," and every baby has his or her small group of disciples to teach. It's hard to hate in your heart when you are holding a baby in your arms. When the baby is sick you learn about faith. A sick child soon brings parents into deep prayer. How many feuds between in-laws have been dissolved as the family came together around the new baby! Our kinship with God seems very real when we have a part in the creation of life ourselves. We know that somehow God is in what we have done. I guess God knew this too. He knew how a baby would teach and how a baby works miracles, so he came to us himself in a baby. Never has a child inspired so much love in so many.

The new baby reawakened my faith. I guess the years make us all skeptics. After all, we've run into all kinds of people. Dishonesty and callousness which we didn't believe could exist have brushed us here and there. We have seen the seamy side. What we haven't experienced for ourselves we have experienced through television and movies and the daily news. Our sensitivities have been battered until every morning when we wake up we put on armor against the onslaught of the world. Then this child is born to us and we are captured by weakness. It is awesome and frightening to be in the presence of genuine innocence. We hardly know how to handle it. We feel unsure of ourselves. We are made vulnerable by our wonder.

Harold Kohn remembers how when he was sixteen he hitchhiked many miles to see his older sister in the hospital where she had given birth to her first child. The infant was brought from the nursery to its mother while the boy stood at the bedside lost in awe. He marveled at this pink nameless little creature, at the button nose and the tulip lips, the dark eyes and the shell-like ears, and those fragile fingers and toes all in their proper places. His sister suddenly asked, "Would you like to hold the baby?" Surprised and unsure in his teen-age clumsiness, he took the infant in his arms and held her close to him. He writes, "It was one of the most memorable moments of my youth, an instant seasoned with a touch of fear and tinge of fascination and mystery, and thoroughly blended with joy." (*The Tinsel and the Hay,* pp. 26f.; Tidings, 1968.)

At Christmas, when we recall all those images of shepherds and Wise Men, the mother Mary, and her child in the straw, I wonder if Mary sensed the yearning of the shepherds and suddenly asked, "Would you like to hold the baby?" Perhaps that is the question for all of us at Christmas:

"Do you want to hold the Baby?" We are drawn away from our skepticism with a touch of fear, a tinge of fascination and mystery thoroughly blended with joy. Of course, the innkeeper had no room for him, and Herod lurks in the ugly shadows. Villains just make it all more real. We know how to deal with villains. We know how to handle them. But how do you deal with this child? What do you do with his weakness? How do you handle his helplessness?

Now that I am a grandfather I think I see how fragile the baby really is, more than I realized as a father. I hadn't seen many babies before we had our own, and to me they were scary creatures. They were all alike and I really didn't like to hold or touch them. Then we had our own. First I learned to hold her, and then I began to see that every baby is an individual. They are all different, each one. Gradually I saw how fragile they are. So many are broken by sickness; even more are broken by the skepticism of the world. Yet in all that fragility there is power. The power of weakness in a baby is overwhelming. This helpless babe commands the whole family. Educated, purposeful adults, powerful in their own right, all bow and coo and wonder and revise their lives and jump to do anything they can for this helpless child. Paul wrote to the Corinthian congregation, "God chose what is foolish in the world to shame the wise, God chose what is weak in the world to shame the strong" (I Cor. 1:27). Is God getting to me in the weakness of this baby? I think so.

Recently an interesting phenomenon happened. It has happened before, but I don't remember when it has ever happened so often in a short time. Five couples, none of whom were members of our church, called at various times to have their babies baptized. Several of them were not at all sure what baptism means, but they told me of a new awareness of God in their lives. Somehow God had come to them in their babies and they wanted to *do* something about it. Their need for faith had been awakened. In the presence of this weakness we become meek, and when we become meek God captures us! His Holy Spirit has been waiting to flood in if we would only open the door. My redemption, my salvation, my fulfillment is no longer a question of searching but rather of finding. It's no longer a matter of my pursuit but a matter of my surrender to the One who is everywhere present. I didn't know that; I ran after salvation. I pursued happiness like the elusive butterfly. But I can't pursue a baby! There is no defensiveness, no running away so that you have to give chase. I find myself captured by its weakness. This little person totally trusts me, and I let my defenses down as I respond with trust, while God slips in and whispers, "Now, believe also in me." The new baby awakens my faith.

The new baby rekindles my hope. Christmas is the festival of lights. The energy crisis calls our attention to how many lights we have been turning on. Which department store can outblaze the other, which house can win the competition for the most brilliant and colorful decorations, at least in the minds of passing motorists? Too much light blinds our sensitivity to light and color. I'm weary of so many competing lights at Christmas. I need One Light to show me the Way, and too often that Christmas Light has become little more than a shadow of a figure who long since passed by. What good is a hope that only lives in the memory, that is only a distant echo? Somehow a new baby at Christmas focuses on the One who is *now,* the one light that shines into that family circle. Everyone gathers around the baby's crib and attention is focused there. It is unifying, peaceful; we are all one again around this child. There is hope in that. I'm ready for something that unifies my life.

The Babe of Bethlehem does this for us. At Christmas we find ourselves gathered around this one focus, Jesus. We are one family here, brothers and sisters. That brings us hope. Even those who cannot accept the Christ of Galilee teaching and healing, even those who cannot accept the Christ of Jerusalem loving, bleeding, dying, rising, can accept the Babe of Bethlehem. We find ourselves together around him.

The other evening a group of us sat in one family's living room and experienced this oneness around Jesus. Our ages were from five to seventy. The kids strung popcorn and cranberries and everyone sang carols. The mother told the Christmas story while young and old carried it out with figurines from the crèche. It was a beautiful, loving experience and we were one there around the baby. The baby brings us all hope.

I think that as a grandparent I see in a baby a second chance for the world. That's not a new thought to us. It crossed my mind as a father. But in our own children we see so many other things. We see the responsibility for their physical care, the change in our own routines to accommodate the baby, the extension of our own dreams and egos. For me as a grandfather, a lot of that clutter is absent and I am freer to see new hope for the future. The awful evil which builds up around us is reversed for a little while in this grandchild. We are thrown back to innocence. The baby starts over fresh and takes us back with her to a new beginning. There is hope in new beginnings.

Then, too, I feel that I will have an important role to play in this new life. I remember the positive influence my grandparents had in my life. The apostle Paul wrote to the young man Timothy, saying, "I am reminded of your sincere faith, a faith that dwelt first in your grandmother Lois" (II Tim. 1:5). Grandparents have a unique opportunity to relate. A child isn't stuck with his grandparents all the time. Their visits are almost 100 percent happy occasions. A child doesn't have to fight for his independence with his grandparents. That means the defenses don't have to be so high. On the other hand, grandparents can be more relaxed than parents. They are just enough removed from the scene to affirm the good in the child without being drawn into the negatives. Grandparents have better hearing, too, I think, in spite of age. Grandparents have seen enough of life to know that the younger generation has some important things to say. Grandparents have their egos, it is hoped, pretty well established. They don't have to be caught in that battle. And grandparents have seen enough of their own children's inconsistencies to have rapport with the grandchildren. Grandparents have been through enough themselves to know that all things do work together for good and that God has unheard of ways of resolving impossible situations. All that builds hope and patience. As a grandfather, I think that when it comes to babies and their meaning my vision is clearer than it has ever been.

The new baby renews my love. In counseling with young couples before marriage, we talk about their plans for children. Most couples say that they plan to spend a few years just sharing life together before they begin their child-raising. They are right to do that. Whenever I hear this my own mind races back to our first year of marriage and the power of love so intimate, so fulfilling, overcoming the loneliness. That first year was a real lark. But soon we found that our love outgrew the two of us. It could not be contained within our one-to-one relationship. Of course, we could share ourselves with others, with family and friends, and with society.

But that does not allow the intimacy of body and mind and soul which is provided by marriage and the family. So we created a child to love in these deeper dimensions. I have often thought to myself that perhaps this is why God created humanity in the first place. His love could not be contained. It reached out and formed another person who could be loved and who could love in return. The divine power of love will be expressed, and this baby of ours was the tangible expression of that love. We had three children, each one the overflow of our love. Now this grandchild brings it all to us again, and more, for we are deeper persons. We have grown in the years with our own children. We are not the same persons they knew. We bring a new dimension to this baby of theirs and she calls out a new dimension in us. Our love is renewed because in this grandchild, as once in our own child, love has come within reach, tangible, touchable.

When I was a child I needed a father that I could get hold of. My dad traveled a lot, but I cannot remember at a feeling level the long weeks he was gone. What I remember, and what I still feel today, are the wonderful days when he was home: How we would wrestle and roughhouse all over the living room floor. How I grew in strength as a teen-ager until at last I could match him. What pleasure I took in knowing I could match him and what greater pleasure I took in knowing I couldn't beat him. I remember the spring vacations when he took me with him on one of his sales trips. I remember the Saturdays in the basement with our heads together working on the electric train. My father's love was touchable.

I have very little use for a heavenly Father up there somewhere in the starry skies. That vague phrase "Somebody up there loves me" really turns me off, because I need a Father I can touch. As we had children, love began to

focus more clearly in them. Now that I am a grandfather
love is renewed again, love that is touchable—love that
came November first in Kristin; love that came down at
Christmas in the Baby Jesus.

Amy Leyden was seven years old and a second-grader.
She wrote her own prayer book because she said she
couldn't understand the big words in her Roman Catholic
prayer book. It has been published as a Christmas card (Our
Sunday Visitor, Inc., Press, Huntington, Inc., 1973). In it
she describes the birth of Jesus this way: "There was a lady
named Mary and Mary married a gie named Joe. And Mary
was going to have a baby . . . so Joe and Mary found a
donkey and it took a night to get to Bethlehem. But it was
so crowded so then they found a stable and in that stable
they found a manger. Then Mary felt a quiver. And the
exsiding thing was Mary had her baby. And above that
stable they saw a star and a shepherd boy came from a sheep
pen. . . . Angels came too. . . . Joseph was thinking how he
wood teach Jesus to hammer. And Mary was thinking of
how wonderful it was when Jesus was born in a stable because nobody else was born in a stable. . . . Jesus was
thinking of how come he had a halo on his head."

And I am thinking, "How come the Christmas Child
brings me so much new joy this year?" Surely, because God
has come to me anew with faith, hope, and love in the flesh
of our own grandchild. Christmas is for children and grandparents. So the tears come more quickly and the carols have
more meaning.

The other evening, our district ministers and wives were
together for our annual Christmas party. We closed it by
singing "Silent Night," and then there was a full minute of
silence. As we were singing, some jet fighter planes came

over, four waves of them, with loud, ominous, long-lasting roars. The song went on, almost drowned out:

> "Son of God, love's pure light,
>   Radiant beams from thy holy face,
>   With the dawn of redeeming grace,
>   Jesus, Lord, at thy birth."

Then we were quiet. The jets roared again and faded. We were silent, and the silence won. The machines of war were gone. The peace of God won out over the noise of man. The weakness of God in a baby shames the strong and overwhelms our lives with new faith and hope and love. Thank you, God, that you come to us so wonderfully in a new baby.

Chapter 9

Graduation Day

All of us have been to someone's graduation exercises. The ceremony is a high moment for everyone concerned. Jesus' graduation day was no less exciting. Having reached the age of twelve, he was considered a man, responsible, "a son of the law." At that significant point in his life, Jesus and his family made a trip to Jerusalem to attend the Passover feast. It was his first trip to the Temple as a "man," his "graduation exercise."

On the way home to Nazareth, Jesus' parents discovered that their son was not in the caravan. Can't you feel the anxiety that must have come over them? It was a family drama, much like those we have in our families today. Jesus grew up in a family circle in which he "became strong, filled with wisdom; and the favor of God was upon him" (Luke 2:40).

I can vividly imagine the growing Jesus as he took journeys alone in the hills around Nazareth. He climbed, explored, and ran; he prayed and thought and dreamed. The hills of Nazareth overlook the Plain of Esdraelon which was red with the blood of many wars. In fact, so much conflict had taken place on that plain where trade routes crossed that the Scriptures suggest God's final battle with the devil will be fought there as well. On the main roads which intersect that plain the Romans used to crucify their political prisoners for everyone to see. As a child, Jesus may have seen these crucifixions, seen what people do to other people.

From the beginning, however, Jesus was surrounded by a family. He could always go home where there was love to balance what he experienced in the world. It isn't enough to be alone and run in the hills with your friends. His mother was there to teach him every day. The synagogue class was there to give him his studies, and Joseph was there to give him a father image as they worked side by side at their trade. I cannot hear Jesus speak of the Father in heaven without thinking of Joseph. What a man he must have been! Then, somewhere along the line, Joseph died. Jesus, the eldest, took up the support of his mother and brothers and sisters until he was thirty.

When I was growing up at home there was a place of solitude for me. It was my own room. I was born and raised in the city of Chicago where life teemed on every side, yet I could go into my room and close the door and be alone. There I was free to think, to pray, to struggle, to assimilate my experiences of the world. It was my castle, and my parents respected my personhood. They knocked for permission to enter. In that room I read, listened to music, wrote diaries and love letters and poems and stories. Sometimes the weight of the world's hurt was so heavy that I would weep and cry out to God. I was free to do this in my castle—to be "me." I could dream, and the fantasies of a thousand worlds were opened from that room. Then in a moment I could step out into the family circle and leave the dream world behind for the real world of love and growth, struggle and learning. There were long talks with my mother. She was at home after school and in the evenings, available for me to ask questions or to cry upon when I had no friends or when my dog was run over. In the summers we left the city and went to my grandparents' home on Lake

Michigan. There I would explore the pine forests, run bare-
foot and free over the sand dunes, sit for long hours day-
dreaming, create treasure hunts, or study the waves and the
sandbars. Wherever we went, winter and summer, there
was the church, with its gentle teaching about Jesus, the
hymns, the fellowship, the assurance of a God who was real
and unchanging. I grew strong in body and in closeness to
God.

Today it is increasingly hard to provide this kind of atmosphere for our children. Even summer camping trips
become hectic. Vacations mean fighting the crowds and
trying to see too much in too short a time. An increasing
number of our children never get out of the city, sometimes
not even out of their neighborhoods. We should make
every effort to enable children and youth to go to summer
camps. Crowded quarters and the high cost of housing make
it almost impossible for children to have their own rooms,
their own private castle, which says to them, "You are
important, important enough to have your own place!" I
still think parents should make every effort to give each
child a room of his own, a room to be alone in when he or
she chooses. Not isolation, just privacy; room to grow.

There are so many pressures today causing the family to
break up or parents simply to become passive about their
children's development. Far too many parents cannot seem
to love their children in a way that is vital for their healthy
development. It isn't giving children the material things that
makes the difference, but giving them your time, giving
them yourselves. David Wilkerson of Teen Challenge, after
ten years of experience in working with teen-age delin-
quents and drug addicts, wrote a book called *Parents on Trial*
(Hawthorn Books, Inc., 1967). It should be required reading for every young married couple. He speaks there of

"the parental curtain of silence" which drops the minute one begins to seek for the truth about why a child became delinquent. In every case parents say, "What did I do to deserve this?" when they should be asking, "Where did I fail?" Loud are the protests that they did all they could; but few are the admissions of selfishness, apathy, lack of discipline, and being too busy to listen, to be present, to take time.

Cornell psychologist Urie Bronfenbrenner has put together piles of statistics which lead him to say, "The system for making human beings in this society is breaking down" (*Psychology Today,* June, 1975, p. 32). He documents the progressive fragmentation and disintegration of the family and shows that nearly every factor having to do with the well-being of children is on the skids.

Another book records the conversations of American youth. It is called *The Music of Their Laughter,* but it is not very musical and it certainly is not laughable. These youths tell of broken, strife-torn families, empty houses for school children to come home to, easy money to buy easy trouble, loveless adult lives for children to model, parents who have abdicated responsibilities, children who grow up never learning the wonder and urgency of human life, and a constant emphasis upon the pleasure of the flesh and an ignorance of the pleasures of the spirit. One man told a friend of his, "We lost our first child." His friend replied, "I didn't know that she was dead!" "Oh," replied the father, "she isn't dead. I was too busy." (Roderick Thorp and Robert Blake, *The Music of Their Laughter;* Harper & Row, Publishers, Inc., 1970.)

A young son was brought before a judge to be sentenced for forgery. The judge had been a friend of the boy's father, and said, "Young man, do you remember your father, the father whom you have disgraced?" "I remember him very well," the boy replied. "When I went to him for advice or companionship he would say, 'Run along, boy, can't you see I am busy reading?' Well, Your Honor, my father finished reading his book, and here I am."

A college girl wrote a letter to *Time* magazine (December 22, 1967) in which she said: "Thank you for the excellent essay, 'On Being an American Parent.' I love my parents and I know they love me, but they've ruined my life. . . . I could never tell my parents anything. It was always, 'I'm too busy . . . too tired . . . that's not important . . . that's stupid . . . can't you think of better things . . . or your friends are wrong.' As a result I stopped telling my parents anything. All communications ceased. We never had that very important thing—fun!"

Where did the idea ever arise that to be a Christian is to be joyless and dull? Surely not from the Lord whose company was eagerly sought by all sorts of people. He was always interested in others, always had time to be really with them. Still we find that home is probably the most difficult place for any Christian to put his faith to work. It is so much easier to be loving and gentle with people we see only once in a while. But we don't fool the people who share our home. What we are at home is what we really are. Home is the place to test how far we have really come in this new life with Jesus Christ. It was in the family circle that Jesus himself grew in wisdom and stature and favor with God and man.

The account in the third Gospel goes on to make a shocking revelation: Jesus rebelled against his parents! After the festival in Jerusalem was over, there was a family misunderstanding. The caravan of pilgrims going north was spread out, with the men in front and behind for protection, and the women and children in the middle. In this case, Mary thought that her young man was with Joseph and the men; Joseph thought his youngster was with Mary and the women. That night in camp, when the families got together, they discovered Jesus was missing. Every parent can identify with their anxiety. We've all had our share of fear and worry, those lonely trips in search of children who didn't come home when they were expected, or those sleepless hours waiting for their return. What a painful process we parents go through, letting children go out on their own. There are years of heart tugs and tears while we cut them loose to make their own way. Mary and Joseph searched the campsites. Perhaps he was with his cousins; but no. Then the sleepless night, waiting until the dawn when they could start the day's journey back to Jerusalem to see where he was.

At last they found him in the Temple with a group of priests and elders, discussing theological questions. It is a mistake for us to picture a precocious boy dominating a cluster of wise men. Hofmann's well-known painting of Jesus standing erect in the midst of listening elders and expounding the truth to them has given us the wrong impression. Luke reports something much simpler: "[He was] in the temple, sitting among the teachers, listening to them and asking them questions" (Luke 2:46).

Then comes the generation gap. Mary runs over to him: "Son, why did you do this to us? Your father and I have been terribly worried trying to find you." Doesn't that sound as though it were taken right out of a modern home? Jesus answers with profound significance: "Why did you have to look for me? Didn't you know that I had to be in my Father's house?" Then Luke adds another note familiar to us parents: "But they did not understand what he said to them."

It is so hard for us parents to trust our growing children with thoughts and decisions of their own. We adults become so dominating we can't see the wisdom of our children. Our own egos become so invested in our offspring that we can hardly allow them the freedom to be individuals in their own right. Of course, to give them that is a sacrifice. It means cutting out part of our soul and handing it to them as a gift. It means taking risks. After all, they may not go the road we want them to go.

As a Christian, I have found it possible to make this sacrifice only when I affirm over and over again that our children are really God's children more than ours. He loves them more than I do and he is actively reaching out to care for them through many different media beside me. Our children are my joy because I have found fulfillment in loving them and I have found partnership with God in creating them. Beyond this, my children owe me nothing. They owe everything to God, just as I do. We stand together as *his* children. We are grateful together to *him* for the love we share and for the way we mutually encourage and build up one another. But to possess them, to expect a return on our investment—no! They are free to be themselves, to be persons. They are God's children!

Children have to fight for this freedom, not only because we are reluctant to give it but because they need to struggle a great deal before they understand how important their personhood is. I think God planned it that we hold on as tightly as we do because they need to break away from us in tribulation. They need to know how hard it is to win the freedom of standing alone. If it were too easy, their self-confidence would never develop. If we didn't care for them enough to hang on with all our might, then they would have no self-image of importance. It's in that tension between their rebellion and our clinging that they find themselves. It's painful all the way; growth is painful.

Notice carefully this dialogue in the Temple: Mary says, "Your father and I have been . . . trying to find you." Jesus answers, "Didn't you know that I had to be in my Father's house?" See how gently but definitely Jesus takes the name of "father" away from Joseph and gives it to God. This is the struggle of every youth! There comes that moment of awareness when a young person discovers that his parents are not God after all. How tragically often a son or a daughter has to leave home at this point because his or her personhood is at stake! The parents would not give their child the integrity of conscience. At one point, years later, when Jesus' family had come to take him home from the crowd, he would not even go out to see them. "Stretching out his hand toward his disciples, he said, 'Here are my mother and my brothers! For whoever does the will of my Father in heaven is my brother, and sister, and mother.'" (Matt. 12:49–50.)

We parents must remember that we are not God! It is our natural inclination to pretend that we are, to hide behind our masks and pretend to be what we are not. Our children see through all of that. They know us as we really are, and we need to know that they know! Our children need to hear us say, "I'm sorry . . . I was wrong." They need the opportunity to forgive us, their parents, in our failures. They need to hear mother and dad say to each other, "I was wrong. Please forgive me." How can they ever learn the joy of forgiveness if we are always perfect and insist it is always the children who need to be forgiven? How can they ever know the freedom of admitting their failures and trusting God to pick up the pieces if we as parents are never free to admit our failures and let our children love us in our weaknesses?

Jesus pointed his earthly parents beyond themselves to the Father, God. He insisted on being a person who stood alone and responsible before the Father of us all. He graduated not only from the synagogue school but from the family circle. Only then was he free to return and be "obedient to them." Luke tells how they all returned to Nazareth and Jesus "was obedient to them." Every child and youth has the choice of whether he will obey and respect his or her parents or not. But, before that, every parent has the choice of whether he or she will relate to God and his family in a way that will cause the children to want to love and respect the parents.

Recently we entered one of those new periods of family life. Our only son graduated from college and went on to seek a job. Between those events he was home for a little over twenty-four hours—long enough to check in for some advice, to pick up the car which was our combination graduation and wedding gift to him, to get his few remaining things, and drive off to his fiancée in California to prepare for a wedding later in the summer. His mother and I waved over the back gate as he turned the corner. He was out from under our wings. Then we went in and cried together, and talked as parents do, and reminisced, and hoped for the future.

We know that we shall have him back in a way richer than ever before—as a man. Like Mary we will keep all the things of his childhood in our hearts. No one can take those from us. We have given him all we can. We shall stand back now, as we have been learning to do, and watch him grow in wisdom and stature and favor with God and man. When he returns to the family circle with his bride, the love and respect for each other will be greater than ever; love and joy will increase.

May we all affirm our families and rejoice in the tensions and the struggles, where each member finds his or her uniqueness before God and in love serves the needs of the others.

Chapter 10

Is This
the Lost Generation?

Recently we spent a holiday in our mountain retreat on the East Verde River with another family from our congregation. It is wilderness country, and late in the afternoon of our first day I was fishing with the college lad who was one of our guests. We were twenty miles from the nearest paved road, deep into the national forest. The ancient trees arched over our heads and that glorious freshness of sight and sound and smell from the damp woods tingled our senses. The native trout were biting for me, but not for my fellow fisherman, so he began to walk back toward the cabin. He found himself passing the camp of four young adults who had backpacked in to this spot. As soon as he came near them they asked if he wanted to share "a joint" —a marijuana cigarette.

This episode seemed symbolic of the universal presence of marijuana in our society. From all reports and from my own observations, every sector of our society is permeated by the drug known as pot, hay, weed, grass, and other slang names. Virtually every person from fourteen to thirty has at least been exposed to marijuana. A high percentage of them have used it. The largest group of young users are "tasters." They are curious and try it out. Another large group use marijuana for social and recreational purposes, much as their parents use alcohol at social gatherings. A smaller group of adolescents and young adults have become dependent on its use.

Marijuana is in a category by itself. I am not referring to any of the other drugs, which make the subject more complex. Information is available to anyone who wants it. I am addressing only the subject of marijuana. You can learn what the researchers know about it in numerous publications and articles. My purpose is to suggest to you as Christ's people why a Christian will probably choose to "keep off the grass."

Today's young people, born in the 1950's and 1960's are said to be "the lost generation." By that I mean they are cut loose from foundations and anchors, adrift on a sea with no land in sight. Near the spot where those young people were camping on Memorial Day is a major hiking trail which snakes along under the Mogollon Rim of Arizona. On vacations I sometimes take that trail out of our canyon and let it lead me a couple of miles over into an isolated canyon which has a creek with brook trout. The trail is blazed with great wounds which have been cut into the trees. Some are so healed from the decades that new ones have to be cut. But others have gone that way before, and by watching for their marks you can't miss the trail. Several times I have tried shortcuts, leaving the trail and striking out through the trees and over the mountains on my own. It always ends in disaster: clothes torn by thick manzanita groves, exhausted from more ups and downs than necessary. The trailblazers knew to go around the head of a canyon and not down and up again and again. When I go off the trail I always get lost and never quite recover a true direction. I usually end up following the canyons down until I am back at the river where I began. By then it's too late in the day to reach my goal. But oh how good it is to get back to the stream of living water and once again see the trail marks on the trees!

People under thirty often have this feeling of being lost in a wilderness where the trail marks have long since been left behind. There is no path to lead them out because no one has gone that way before to blaze the trail. We who were born before 1945 cannot possibly share the insecurities of those who were born since then. They have never known a day when the end of the world was not an imminent possibility. The conventional wars and the Great Depression of my generation bound our families together in love and mutual support. But my children and their generation have lived from birth under the double threat of planet-wide disaster and an affluence which has torn families apart. They have never experienced the security of two or three generations living and working together in the same kind of world. The world as my children experience it has never been the world as I experience it. To live and work together at all, we have had to teach each other about our respective worlds. I would hate to think of where our family would be if we did not have the love of Jesus Christ on which to find our common ground.

So this is the "lost generation." It's not that they drop out, it's just that they never had a chance to get tuned in. Drugs seem to help to fill the emptiness. In this group of adolescents and young adults we find more feelings of separation and alienation, loneliness and rejection, than in any generation in history. It is understandable that these persons should rebel against the institutions. Governments don't keep the peace or promote the general welfare as they were created to do. Schools don't prepare them for life or guarantee them a means of earning a living. Homes do not provide love and security. Churches don't bring them into the presence of God. These are generalizations, of course. But this is how many of our youth have experienced the institutions of society. They do not do it for them! Is it any wonder that they reject these institutions and feel rejected by them? They have sought elsewhere for meaning and fulfillment.

Youthful drug use has been called both a barometer and a commentary on our society. It reflects the failure of our institutions, notably the family, to enable our children to discover fulfillment and self-realization. We talk about the drugs and addiction until it becomes a smoke screen against the real trouble in our own homes.

Any thinking person can see through the bankrupt morality and hypocrisy of today's mainline American society. When youth see adults take cigarettes for the nicotine, tranquilizers to calm them down, diet pills to slim them, other pills to keep them alert, drinks to keep them going, sleeping pills at night, and aspirin by the truckload, it is fair to say we have raised them in a drug-oriented society. There is a game some teen-agers have been known to play called "Salad Bowl." Each young person at the party brings a collection of pills and capsules from the family medicine chest. These are mixed up in a bowl and each person takes a handful as though eating salted peanuts. Obviously this is the next thing to playing Russian roulette.

Parents panic over their kids' smoking pot, yet over one billion gallons of beer, liquor, and wine are poured down American throats every year. At least six million of our citizens are alcoholics, causing uncounted damage to homes and loved ones and the economy. One third to one half of all arrests in America involve drunkenness. Cirrhosis is the sixth leading cause of death; 20 percent of the inmates in state mental hospitals are there because of irreversible alcoholic brain damage; 50 to 70 percent of the deaths and injuries each year from auto accidents involve alcohol. Yet not only is alcohol legal but it is pushed as a major national industry.

How can a teen-ager, still trying to discover who he or she is, handle the rigid hypocrisies of the elders? He can't even have a reasonable discussion with them about drugs. Finally we can talk about sex with our kids. We are beginning to talk with them about death. But drugs we can't handle, probably because we're too guilty. We parents panic and our overreaction pushes our youth back toward drugs and the drug culture. At least there they are accepted and their behavior is not censured. Where else can they turn?

Another major hypocrisy is the way we talk about our love for them while our children don't experience love. The drive for affluence and status leaves our children parentless. I've discovered that a child from a divorced home or an orphan who gets real adult attention has a better chance for health and fulfillment than a child from a "normal" home where the parents are so permissive that there are no hard lines or clear standards against which to react. Permissiveness makes the world seem like jello: soft, insecure, loose. Parents who are so busy making money, chasing pleasure, and doing good works that they are never available to give their children adult companionship will lose their children, probably to the drug scene.

It is increasingly clear to me that we have robbed our children of their childhood. The urban complex has closed in so that we can't let them run free for a day. Our drive for them to achieve parallels our own drive for economic success. We push them into lessons of all sorts, we insist on academic excellence, we fill their social calendar, setting ourselves as examples. We insist on all sorts of regimented sports activities and competition. We also like to have them off our backs so we can pursue our own pleasures and projects. Instead of monitoring the television viewing, we allow them endless hours of exposure to violence and seduction. Between television and the treadmill of extracurricular activities, there is no time left to play or to develop the imagination. No time left to play! Scientists have discovered that a child who walks too soon and does not crawl has stunted the development of his brain at a vital age. For therapy, grown children and adults are having to go back and crawl, crawl until the brain can pick up that vital experience without which the adult is not a whole person. We have allowed a worse thing to happen when we rob children of the opportunity to develop the ability to imagine. Taking drugs is a desperate attempt to release an undeveloped imagination. Instead, what is released is a Pandora's box of horrors.

We are beginning to see a generation of adolescent adults, eighteen- to thirty-year-olds who can't settle down and make a contribution to society, who turn to marijuana for new experiences because they never completed their childhood. They didn't play enough, were not free enough to explore, to imagine, to dream, to develop the wonderful capacity to be timeless, without artificial means.

If we were to use the language of religion, we would say that these young people need salvation. If we were to use the language of psychology, we would talk about their human need for integration, identity, health, fulfillment, and purpose. If anyone is to have a full life, he or she must have a sense of well-being and peace, an assurance that life has meaning, a knowledge that people are part of a community. If a person can't find these things "within the system," that person deliberately withdraws from society and forms a society with like-minded others. This is a life-or-death matter. It is a search for salvation.

We use a word in Christian theology—*atonement*. It describes what Jesus does by his death on the cross. It is really two words put together: "At" and "one"—at-one-ment. Salvation, or the fulfilled life, is achieved by some act of at-one-ment, some act which bridges the separation and makes us one again. There are three or four relationships in which we must experience this oneness. To be integrated and healthy we must be at one with ourselves, with others, with God, and with creation. The use of marijuana is one of the most prevalent means by which today's youth try to find at-one-ment. The fellowship around marijuana is powerful, and the weed becomes the point of contact for frightened people reaching out to others. Like the Christians who were thrown together in the catacombs of Rome, smoking together is the place these young people are at one with each other. Like Christians drawing a fish in the dust for mutual recognition, so the question, "Want to share a joint?" is the code for instant identification and common cause. Getting stoned together is parallel to Christians sharing a meal they ritualistically call the Lord's Supper.

There is a better way to be at one with others than through the fellowship of dope. Young people who discover Jesus Christ have found that better way. For one thing, marijuana doesn't really work. Smokers feel more alienated than ever from parents and society. Dope becomes *the symbol* for this separation a youth feels from parents and from institutions. Marijuana and its signs have become the rallying point for the rebellion of youth trying to find their way. Jesus Christ, the Son of God, was a rebel against the existing institutions also. That makes him pretty attractive to youth. When young people come together over their faith in Jesus, they find at-one-ment with each other that doesn't give rise to guilt or escalate their natural rebellion against home and society. Standing with arms around each other and singing, "We are one in the Spirit, We are one in the Lord," crying for joy and love with each other, laughing and working and praying and sharing in Christ— all this has marijuana beat in every way.

Also, the use of marijuana is against the law. Christians always reserve the right to break the law in a passive manner if resistance is necessary for the general welfare. But to break the law for personal pleasure is not something our Lord ever lets us do. Even passing a joint from one person to another can land a person in the penitentiary for years. We value our citizenship in this democracy. We want to preserve our record for the sake of our future and our children. We want to be as effective as possible influencing the affairs of our communities. Christians are found constantly weighing the values of every possible action. Marijuana doesn't weigh out well at all. It is not God's will for us to be alienated further from society and the people around us. Christian youth will find oneness with others through Jesus, not through pot.

One April evening, when we were living in California, the telephone exchange of a television and radio station was jammed with 170,000 calls. The callers were persons who had been listening to and watching an hour-long broadcast on drug abuse during which youngsters had informally given terrifying testimony. One young person had said, "I started drugs at eleven; at ten I started smoking cigarettes and drinking wine; at nine I started fighting, and in the third grade I started robbing the school. . . . I was crying out for help. I wanted somebody to say, 'Hey, man, why are you doing that?' . . . I wanted somebody to really care about me."

I could only hope that through someone Christ would look into that fellow's eyes as He had looked into the eyes of His friends another night long ago and say: "As the Father has loved me, so have I loved you; abide in my love. If you keep my Father's commandments, you will abide in my love, just as I have kept my Father's commandments and abide in his love. These things I have spoken to you, that my joy may be in you, and that your joy may be full" (John 15:9–11).

Chapter 11

Please Keep Off the Grass

The fellowship we have in Christ Jesus is the true way to find at-one-ment with each other. The other vital relationships which make up the fulfilled or abundant life are: the relationship with oneself, and the relationship with God and his creation.

When I left home at eighteen and went away to college, I took with me my faith in God. I knew God as a loving Father, but I had never surrendered my life to Jesus as Lord. That meant I was still trying to find myself. There was no mastering force for my life which marshaled all my talents and efforts in a clear-cut direction. We didn't know about marijuana in the '40s, but beer and whiskey became the signs of independence. Getting high, as we called it then too, was our sign to the world that we were on our own, making our own decisions apart from parental authority. The irony was that alcohol rendered us less than human, robbed us of our ability to make judgments, and made us dependent rather than independent. After a year and a half of that I had come far enough in my search for identity that I decided I would belong to Jesus Christ. If I belonged to Christ, then it was his will and not mine which mattered. It was obvious from this new point of view that Christ did not will for me to drink alcohol. I could feel that creeping dependence on the drug. I knew I was hardly capable of serving him when I was drunk. I realized I was gambling with the future since I might easily hurt myself or others. I also realized I was going to influence some other persons to drink who in turn might cause an injury or become alcoholics. The reasons my Lord opposed my drinking alcoholic beverages were beginning to become clear.

Suddenly on February 22, 1948, I became an abstainer. The date is memorable because it was Washington's birthday and our fraternity was having a big bash to celebrate the father of our country. I went to the party determined to abstain, and for the next several months I found myself in an exhilarating debate with my friends about why I no longer drank alcohol. It was one of the great moral victories of my life. It strengthened my new identity. It brought a new depth of peace and harmony with myself. I· belonged to Christ, although that was said softly with well-chosen words at age nineteen in a fraternity house.

If I were to try to find out who I was today, testing myself against my home and society, the route would probably be marijuana. Trying to find at-one-ment with oneself is described today by such phrases as "getting it all together" or "getting my head on straight."

Like alcohol, however, marijuana is a great deceiver. It acts upon the central nervous system and releases inhibitions which normally stand guard over our behavior. At first the smoker is talkative and giggly, but that is followed by a drowsy state of euphoria which is easily confused with peace of mind. The self is actually anesthetized. Conflicts and problems don't matter anymore. Time and space are distorted and sounds are exaggerated. The person who belongs to Christ Jesus will think this through ahead of time, weighing the options and results. Instead of making you one with yourself, marijuana gives a false peace. It is a state in which you have made yourself less than human. The apostle

Paul put it this way in I Cor. 3:16: "Do you not know that you are God's temple and that God's spirit dwells in you? If any one destroys God's temple, God will destroy him. For God's temple is holy, and that temple you are." A few chapters later he says again: "Do you not know that your body is a temple of the Holy Spirit within you, which you have from God? You are not your own; you were bought with a price. So glorify God in your body" (I Cor. 6: 19–20).

Did you catch the phrase "You are not your own"? It is beautiful to have an identity: to *be* somebody because you belong to somebody—Jesus. The things we Christians have to guard against are those habits and dependencies which creep in to rob us of our identity. The pothead belongs to pot, not Christ.

Eldridge Cleaver in his book *Soul on Ice* (McGraw-Hill Book Co., Inc., 1968) speaks about his first imprisonment at eighteen for possession of marijuana. He says: "I had gotten caught with a shopping bag full of marijuana, a shopping bag full of love—I was in love with the weed and I did not for one minute think that anything was wrong with getting high." I know a young married man who buys marijuana even though his wife goes without shoes. He insists he's not addicted; he claims he doesn't *have* to smoke, but he does. I am reminded of the alcoholic's protests of innocence or the cigarette smoker's insistence that he can stop anytime. To prove it, he stops many times every day.

From what we know scientifically it is not correct to say that marijuana is addictive. We say instead that it creates a dependency. It may be a psychological dependency, but for practical living it's the same either way. It means you have to have it. *It* rules your life, not Christ, not your better judgment yielded to Christ. An increasing number of twenty- and thirty-year-olds who have been smoking marijuana for five years or more are showing signs of becoming what one doctor calls "potaholics" or "grassaholics." Dr. Jordan Scher says that these patients have what is called a compulsion to use marijuana. He adds, "You may call it psychological if you wish, but as far as I am concerned, it is a considerably stronger and urgent force."

Call it what you will, marijuana disrupts any good relationship with yourself and steals your freedom to think clearly, to develop your potential, to make intelligent choices, or be an agent of God's Holy Spirit. Psychological measurements prove that thinking under the influence of pot is inaccurate and that concentration and manual dexterity are impaired. However, the people who took the tests *thought* their scores had improved taking marijuana, and none of them recognized that their abilities were lowered. The marijuana user often insists it gives him a better understanding of himself; what he really means is a better understanding of the drug experience. The experience is what becomes most important—not his personal growth and development.

The search for salvation through marijuana is the search for harmony with others and with the self. Now we turn to another relationship—harmony with God and his creation. When John Denver sings about a "Rocky Mountain High" some listeners picture a group of youth sitting around the campfire smoking pot in that glorious natural setting. Many recent songs become hymns to the religious experience induced by marijuana. The drug seems to concentrate the senses so that a sight, a smell, a sound is magnified. One youth told me of staring at a spider web in the forest for a long time until it seemed he was almost one with its beauty. A oneness with nature and with God is something we desperately need for salvation. It is easy to interpret an experience like this, and the absence of life's other problems, to be an experience of God. I dare say every one of us has wished we had a shortcut to God. Marijuana seems like the answer, but it ends in disillusionment. As one Eastern mystic has said, "The drug experience is as far removed from reality as is a mirage from water" (Meher Baba).

What marijuana really does is lower the barriers to input from the world around us that we ordinarily have. In order to live day by day you have to shut out a clutter of sight and sound. Under the influence of the drug these monitors are gone and you experience everything full blast. You also lose the capacity to discriminate between what is meaningful and what is not. This sense of judgment is critical for creative work. Under drugs, creativity seems to be heightened, but it really is not. Artists and musicians and writers working under the influence of drugs think they are doing fantastic things but find later they have produced chaos. One young artist thought that using marijuana and LSD would help him be more creative, so he began using them. Later he said: "The strange thing that I found has to do with the amount of creative work that I could produce. I had a lot of thoughts in my head. I had great ideas about new art forms, but I had nothing actually there. It was still rambling around in the back of my head somewhere, and it wasn't actually coming down my arm and out to my fingers. When I'm on drugs like that, sooner or later my hand starts shaking and the pen falls right out of my hand. That's really a bummer, because you can't get anything accomplished if it is all in your head. The role of the artist is to present to the public what's in your head!"

The testimony of many who have been through this drug scene, like Dr. Allan Cohen, who was formerly an associate of Timothy Leary, is that the "Turn on, tune in, drop out" theme of the drug cult is a false religion. It never does make better people, Cohen says. Marijuana users often talk about love and brotherhood and God, but in fact they do not live more spiritual lives. The drug only makes them think they are very spiritual people.

One of the most serious problems for the marijuana smoker is apathy, which doesn't bring him closer to God and nature but actually separates him from them further. God created human beings to be his partners and cocreators. Apathy is treason in the Kingdom of God. Instead of putting one in harmony with God, the pot-smoker is actually at war with God. One young fellow broke through to this discovery and decided to put dope out of his life. He said, "Nobody can change society loaded," and then, realizing that social change is pretty hard even when the best of talents is sober, he added: "My society may not change, but I can. I can develop and grow, and I can help others change and grow. The goal, maybe, is not so much to create a better world as it is to create better people in the world." I like that. It gets down where I can handle it.

Most clinicians now agree that to grow and develop or to help others grow is almost an impossibility for chronic pot-smokers. Regular users lose their motivation. They prefer a non-goal-oriented life-style which emphasizes immediate pleasures to the exclusion of ambition or planning. Normal adolescence is a time of psychological turmoil without drugs. It is a time when youths wrestle with life and learn how to cope with reality. But the marijuana-user wards off reality and develops a pattern of avoiding real self-development, those all-important relationships to self, others, and God.

All this borrows on the future. Belonging to Christ

means to me, among other things, that the future is God's. It is his gift to me. I trust him with it, and if I do anything to belittle or cripple that future I have robbed myself and the world of great blessings. I have also cheated God. This applies to the matter of apathy. If I am lulled by "grass" to not move through the doors of opportunity God has set before me, the results can be devastating to the future. When a President's son, Jack Ford, told a nationwide television audience that he had smoked marijuana, a United Methodist pastor in North Carolina, Kenneth Johnson, preached an open letter to him. The pastor said: "Like your father, I admired your candor. I was pleased that you gave a direct response to the matter. With a few days to reflect upon your statement, however, I would like to take a few minutes of your time to respond. . . . First, are you not on shaky ground scientifically when you compare the effects of marijuana-smoking to beer-drinking and wine-drinking? According to a consensus of authorities . . . we know the results of beer and wine upon the body, but the jury is still out on the effects of marijuana."

What he means is that we just don't know yet what long-term physical effects the chronic use of marijuana may produce. The drug was introduced in the United States in 1920. By 1937 it was outlawed by federal and state governments. Its active ingredient was not produced in pure form until 1966, and only now for the first time are researchers able to measure and study its long- and short-term effects, possible organ damage, and other results. To take the chance is surely gambling with the future.

As a Christ-person it isn't simply my own future that I would be gambling with, but God's future. A National Institute of Mental Health brochure states: "A person using marijuana finds it harder to make decisions that require

clear thinking. And he finds himself more easily open to
other people's suggestions. Doing any task takes good
reflexes, and thinking is affected by the drug. For this reason
it is dangerous to drive while under the influence of the
drug."

The Rev. Mr. Johnson, in his sermon to the President's
son, concluded: "Are you not on shaky ground Biblically in
your position? Somewhere in your religious upbringing I'm
sure you were taught that you are your brother's keeper."
Jack Ford wrote the preacher and thanked him.

"Truly, truly, I say to you [said Jesus], he who does not
enter the sheepfold by the door but climbs in by another
way, that man is a thief and a robber." (John 10:1.) Marijuana is not the door to the presence of God. Anything that
has control over me, or anything which when taken renders
me less than in full control of my abilities, is suspect. It is
a lie to say that marijuana puts me in touch with God or in
any way makes me a better person. It so alters my powers
of reason and sense, it so clogs my spiritual pipeline to God,
that I seem to be alive and sensitive when in fact I have been
robbed of life and creativity. Motivation, growth, and
meaning come out of tensions and conflicts. Marijuana takes
a person out of the tension so that he does not have to
resolve the dilemmas or face the paradoxes. It is cheap grace
—an escape. Marijuana is a thief and a robber. Instead of
discipline, instead of learning from pain and experience,
instead of meeting each hour with the fullest capacity to
serve and be creative, pot covers a person with a shroud of
unreality and ineffectiveness.

Jesus goes on to say: "I am the door; if any one enters
by me, he will be saved, and will go in and out and find
pasture. The thief comes only to steal and kill and destroy;

I came that they may have life, and have it abundantly"
(John 10:9–10).

The world needs strong, creative, determined, motivated
persons, not persons turned in on their own private world
of hallucinations. The commitment of your life to the person of Jesus Christ can put you at one with God, with the
world, with your self, and with others. Marijuana is the
thief, the deceiver, the robber! Christ is the door to the real
thing. Praise him with a clear mind. Serve him with vigor
and determination. Be present with his children who need
you, and need you functioning at your very best.

PART FOUR

Living as a Family

Chapter 12

Honorable Parents

It is a timeless law of life that the fabric of society is woven together with honor for father and mother. When that honor unravels, society unravels. The nation, the land, the civilization goes down and is lost. Fathers and mothers are the mediators of the divine claim on our lives. The parent is the child's first god. Mother and father are the first incarnation we meet and through them God supplies our needs, defends our weaknesses, gives us wisdom and knowledge, and imparts to us conscience and motivation. To honor them is to honor God. Where the child does not honor his parents, neither does he honor God. This is where the foundations of personal and social life are undermined. The parent who is cruel and selfish is the ingredient of the dying civilization. Such parents make it impossible for their children to honor God—the archetype for which the parents stand. Children who do not honor their parents cast their own souls into a living hell because neither can they honor and obey God. Thus Moses communicated one of God's cardinal rules in the Fifth Commandment, "Honor your father and your mother, that your days may be long in the land which the LORD your God gives you" (Ex. 20:12).

A well-known theologian was asked why he believed in God. His unexpected answer was, "Because my mother taught me." That's where it all begins; that is where the seeds of our agonies and our ecstasies are sown. The record tells us that when he was twelve Jesus went with his parents to Nazareth, where he was obedient to them and grew up, both in body and in wisdom (see Luke 2:51–52). Wisdom moves from the outside to the inside. Obedience must be to parents before it can be to conscience. The child does not have the wisdom to understand all of his parents' directives. He has to be saved from his own self-centeredness and his own lack of experience. To this very day I am not wise enough to understand all the directives God gives to me, but when I was a child I learned to trust my parents and believe that their ways were best for me. Thus I grew up learning to trust and honor God. "The fear of the LORD is the beginning of wisdom." (Ps. 111:10.) But until the child is old enough to transfer that loyalty to God, the beginning of wisdom is really the fear of the parent—"fear" in the sense of respect and appreciation and fear also in the sense that "I'm scared of what will happen if I don't obey." That's where it has to begin.

One hot summer evening I was sitting in the congregation of the Great Plains Christian Ashram in Kansas. It was not my turn to speak that night but I was listening to another speaker. Across the open space in the pew sat a mother with her three-year-old lad. The father in that family was away for the week. This little tyke slid across the open space in the pew and touched me; then he slid back to his mother. Soon he had worked over to me again. This time he sat very close and I put my arm around him, but in a minute he moved away again. The next time he worked back to me he climbed up on my knee and then he came on into my lap. I put my arms up around his middle but it was very warm that night and soon I put them back down to my sides. Immediately he reached down and pulled my arms up around him again, put his head back under my chin, and just sort of melted into my body. It was nice for me to be needed and to be trusted. During the closing hymn when we were all standing I leaned over to the mother and said, "Tell this boy's daddy how much he missed him." It is in the security and in the caring of our parents or our parent substitutes that we first learn to trust and honor God, for they are God's agents.

Honor for father and for mother is a most powerful motive for good in our lives. We were reminiscing the other day with a friend who was telling us about his teen-age years in a small Pennsylvania town. He was a daredevil and his pride and joy was a motorcycle which he raced up and down those Pennsylvania hills. He told us that at the top of the hill in the town was a funeral home and every time he came roaring up that way the funeral director would stand out on the front porch and rub his hands together. My friend Frank said that it really was spooky, and when they met in town the funeral director would say, "I'm going to get you one of these days, Frank." That was frightening, but it didn't cause him to stop racing his motorcycle. When he got rid of the motorcycle the reason was not that he was afraid of the danger but that his mother worried about him. It was to honor her that he quit riding the motorcycle.

When people stop smoking it usually has nothing to do with saving their own lives. It is out of concern for the people who love them. Where chastity survives among our young people it has little to do with the fear of pregnancy in this day and age. It has everything to do with honor for father and mother.

It is this honor which points beyond parents to the Kingdom of God. Christian parents know that they point beyond themselves. Jesus said one of those strange and confusing things in this regard. We read in Luke 14:25–26: "Now great multitudes accompanied him; and he turned and said to them, 'If any one comes to me and does not hate his own father and mother and wife and children and brothers and sisters, yes, and even his own life, he cannot be my disciple.' " It's one of those emphatic statements he often used. The Aramaic root of the word "hate" means "to love less." Matthew records another version of the statement: "He who loves mother or father more than me is not worthy of me" (Matt. 10:37). The honor we hold for our parents is the mold from which is cast our honor for God. It all points to him. When the claims of parents and God are in conflict there is no question for the mature person. We must act as if we hated parents, that is, loved them less than God. The disciples left home and parents and followed Christ. Jesus himself had to make this choice. His mother and his brothers came one day to take him home, for they were concerned over his sanity and his safety. But the Kingdom of God had first claim upon him and when they said, "Your mother and your brothers are outside, asking for you." He replied, "Who are my mother and my brothers?" And looking at the people who sat around him, he said, "Here are my mother and my brothers! Whoever does the will of God is my brother, and sister, and mother" (Mark 3:32–35).

Parents and children must let each other go for the higher loyalty. The German pastor Martin Niemoeller suffered in a concentration camp under Hitler. Church people in America felt great sorrow for Niemoeller, but his father sent word to America not to pity Martin. He said that the person to pity was any follower of Christ who did not know the joy reserved for those who are faithful. It was terrible to know that his son suffered in the concentration camp. It would be worse if his son had not been willing to suffer for God.

When a parent honors God like that, no wonder the child grows up to honor God!

Our civilization is coming apart at the seams. As far as I can see, it is because parents have been so dishonorable that the children have never learned to honor them or God! Most parents are not psychotic. They are just lazy and selfish and apathetic. Mothers and fathers rob their children of the assurance that they are loved with a tough love that will last forever when they refuse the discipline and regulation which children and adolescents need. Most of the problem is selfishness. It's a difficult, full-time job to be a parent. It takes work and worry and pain and a lot of inconvenience to rear a child. Far easier to let the child do what he wants —ignore his failures, rationalize his sins, teach him by neglect to be lazy and insolent, or selfish and crude.

There is something of a universal law that the fewer sacrifices we make the more we hesitate to make even those few. We parents can wake up some morning to discover that our luxuries have become necessities, our children are in the way, and our egos have become god. We should also wake up to the fact that by that time the hero has gone out of the home. If there are no heroes in the home, there can be no heroes coming out of the home. No wonder the Fifth Commandment ties the honor of parents together with the promise of the land!

As a pastor I have seen a long trail of parents who are remorseful as they weep over their fallen children. "How could he have done it?" they say of a son almost dead from an overdose. "We never suspected it," they lament about a daughter who is about to give birth and no one is sure about the child's father. There is bewildered disbelief, the heaping of blame onto the children, and an inability to grasp where *they* made any mistakes.

Why is it so hard for us parents to admit that we have failed? The crisis of our civilization is the evidence. Books and magazines are full of guidelines for parents to follow. My own list of suggestions would run something like this: *Be available*—Do not have an empty house for your children to come home to day after day. Make it possible for them to entertain their friends, with your help in the background. *Show appreciation*—Encourage and compliment your children's accomplishments and let them know how important their role is in the family. Express straight-out verbal messages of caring. *Demonstrate affection*—Make overt expressions of your love. When was the last time you hugged your boy or your girl? When was the last time mother and father hugged each other in front of the children? *Express respect*— Assure your children that they are important persons who have the right to privacy. The children's sealed mail and closed doors and secret hearts are their own to share only when they desire. *Maintain discipline*—Be consistent about it, which says you care enough to share the pain and the inconvenience of a punishment, that there is law and order in the universe, and that responsible living is a superior value. *Be waiting to listen*—Always find time to try and understand, to love, to comfort, to care, above and beyond your little projects, which can wait.

One pastor tells of having dinner in a church member's home. He was impressed with the unusually good behavior of the four-year-old boy. Soon he discovered the reason for the child's charm. The mother was at the kitchen sink washing dishes when the little fellow came to her with a magazine and asked, "Mother, what is this man in the picture doing?" She dried her hands, sat down in a chair, took the boy into her lap, and spent ten minutes answering his questions. After the child had left, the pastor commented on the

incident, saying that many mothers would not be inter-
rupted like that. She answered, "I expect to be washing
dishes the rest of my life, but never again will my son ask
me that question."

Being parents our children can honor is the toughest,
most important job of a lifetime, and yet it is performed
entirely by amateurs. By the time we have learned how to
do it, it's all over. It's the only instance of on-the-job training where once you are trained you are dismissed. The only
real preparation we parents have for the job comes from
having been children ourselves. That means we perpetuate
our parents' mistakes and add a few of our own. Either God
has fouled up the process or else the proper techniques and
the professional guidelines really are not the key issue.

I have come to believe that the one real key is love, that
love which is ready to sacrifice and points beyond itself to
God.

> Happy the home when God is there,
>   And love fills every breast;
> When one their wish, and one their prayer,
>   And one their heavenly rest.
>
> Happy the home where Jesus' name
>   Is sweet to every ear;
> Where children early lisp his fame,
>   And parents hold him dear.
>
> Happy the home where prayer is heard,
>   And praise is wont to rise;
> Where parents love the sacred Word
>   And all its wisdom prize.
>   —*Henry Ware, Jr.*

Given that, I don't believe the other differences matter.
Life-styles, economic status, educational levels, personality

differences, philosophies of child-raising—these things can
vary and it doesn't really matter. What matters is that children honor their parents because they see their parents
honor their grandparents. What matters is that they know
that their parents are honorable and that the honor of God
and his law is the supreme value in the home. It's that kind
of home that Edward Bok, the famous Dutch immigrant
who later became the head of Curtis Publications, knew
about. He had inscribed over the fireplace in his home: "It
is so easy to get lost out in the world that I come here to
find myself."

One evening, as parents were picking up their children from our day-care center, I observed one mother
dragging her child by the arm out to the car. The little
fellow was crying and dragging his feet because he
didn't want to go home. Who knows what that mother's
day had been, but she was slapping the child on the
head all the way out to the car and yelling at him, "I'm
not going to go through this with you every night! Shut
up!" When she reached the car she literally threw the
child in with an angry curse and then beat him some
more before she drove off. I was sick in my stomach as
well as my soul from watching this episode. The next
morning, I arrived at my office at the same time this
mother was bringing the child back for the day. I
couldn't believe my eyes. He was holding her hand,
skipping and singing, laughing and talking happily with
her all the way up the walk. He had forgiven her! I had
not. I still seethed. But he had forgiven her! It was a
whole new day.

Our children give us so many chances. We fail time and
time again, but it isn't easy to ruin a child. They are *so*

resilient, so forgiving, and so trusting. Let us pray that we will so honor our fathers and our mothers, and in turn be honorable in our children's sight, that our days may be long in the land which the Lord our God gives to us.

Chapter 13

It Is Harder
to Be a Mother

On south State Street in Chicago is the old Pacific Garden Mission. A painted banner across the chapel wall asserts, "Mother's Prayers Follow You." Thousands of down-and-outers have read that over the decades, many of them turning to Jesus Christ in surrender because of the reminder. It was the memory of mother which stirred Rudyard Kipling to write:

> If I were hanged on the highest hill,
> I know whose love would follow me still,
>   Mother o' mine, O mother o' mine!

> If I were drowned in the deepest sea,
> I know whose tears would come down to me,
>   Mother o' mine, O mother o' mine!

> If I were damned o' body and soul,
> I know whose prayers would make me whole,
>   Mother o' mine, O mother o' mine!

I'm not sure how many people today can respond with that kind of sentiment. So much about the family is changing, and the task of full-time motherhood is often in disrepute. Quite apart from women's liberation and all the protests and new patterns it has produced, there are several other facts that make it harder than ever to be a mother. For one thing, there is no longer a community to help. Not many decades ago, a mother shared her child-raising with neighbors, teachers, father, and the extended family. A child could expect a spanking in any of a dozen homes and also at school if he misbehaved. The whole community took an interest. When I was a preschooler I used to visit in four or five homes on my street. I usually got a second and third breakfast in two of them, a snack at the third, and played the owner's harp at the fourth.

We had friends on a farm in Illinois whose little boy was driving the tractor and the combine at age twelve and had been working beside his dad ever since he could toddle. That day is gone. Father is nowhere around in our times. He goes to some mysterious place every day and often his children don't even know what he does there.

The family is too small now to be the group experience it was when ten people from three generations lived under the same roof. There was a personal exchange possible in those days which enabled one to find identity as a person. It is only in the intimate exchange with other persons that we can know ourselves. Today the elderly or unmarried live alone and do not share in this experience. Family groups include only one, two, or three children, and even they are so mobilized that little face-to-face exchange takes place. The family is no longer the community in which we discover ourselves and learn to live the sensitive life.

This leaves today's mother pretty much alone. She soon becomes a servant without benefit of fellowship. She carries the major portion of child-raising. When father does get home from work he's so exhausted he runs to hide. Mother feels she has to shield him from demanding children and her own heart hungers. The built-in baby-sitters are gone— grandparents, maids, and the line of older children. For all the push-button gadgets, mother still works an eighty-hour week with her higher standards of cleanliness, taxi service for the family, and lack of help from the others. By the end of the day she feels like a pie without enough slices to go around.

In the midst of this life-style a wife and mother would find survival more promising if she had a sharing prayer group to which she could relate. Every one of us must have some community of persons with whom we can be transparent. Our health and well-being depends on having others to whom we can make ourselves known in an atmosphere of caring and acceptance. Consider anger, for example; we all have it. It is a gift, for it releases our emotions. But we mishandle it when we push it down into cold storage. Frozen anger freezes everything else in us. We need to unfreeze it and let it out. This takes a supporting community where we experience grace when we do voice our feelings. We need a group where the truth can be spoken in love, where we can risk exposing our real feelings. Our Lord Jesus Christ created this kind of community in that group of disciples who traveled with him. He said that this kind of love experience is at the heart of the Kingdom of God, that in it we find freedom, joy, peace, and power.

In a time when the family often fails to be the community in which life's fulfillment can happen, we must find new communities. In some places three or four families are banding together either for some sort of communal life, or at least to meet regularly, to share and to serve one another. Others find that the small group becomes the place where the adventure of growth can take place and where each member is built up instead of torn down. The local church can easily form these new communities where Christ is the center. One person said: "I have no family to relate to in this city. They are all in other states. This is the only place

I can come and be myself and be accepted in love." More mothers and fathers, individually or as couples, and more youths are finding that the small group is becoming their new family of support and personal growth where the traditional family is not filling the need.

Not only is there no longer a community to help mother in her basic tasks today, but she is under more pressure than ever to take on additional responsibilities as breadwinner or social worker. An increasing percentage of marriages end in divorce, and a growing number of children are born to unmarried women. Even in normal marriages the increasing demand for additional income has sent mother out of the home to a job. Other significant factors in today's scene include the pressure on women to take on a career outside the home. After all, she is freed from the shackles of ignorance, pregnancy, and male dominance which have traditionally kept women at home. Now she is encouraged to compete. Besides, by age thirty-two (the national average) her last child is in school. Expecting to live into her late seventies, what will she do with this major part of her life still ahead? She feels she must prepare for a career. Those who do not are pressed to meet the growing demands of social welfare. The compassion of women is desperately needed in so many areas of our society. Anyone who shows a willingness to serve is pressured to get into Scouts, church committees, clubs, welfare programs, political causes, hospital volunteers—you name it. Those things are good; someone has to do them! How torn a mother is today by such conflicting demands.

Perhaps the answer for today's mother lies in clarifying life's priorities and arriving at a new understanding of marriage and the home. How does a mother view her family? Commerce sees the family as a consumer; the politician sees it as a vote; the community tends to see it as a resource for worthy projects. All such views make the family a means to some other end. The Christian mother comes to see her family as an end in itself, the arena of God's creative activity, herself a partner with God in the creating. The beginning and end of God is love. Love is something you do, enabling someone else to become the person he or she is capable of becoming. Here is woman's opportunity to decide that her natural position as mother in the family circle is the supreme fact in her life. Making her home a loving, adventuring center for personal growth is supremely more important than a larger income, the excitement of a career, or the glamour of community service. For her to be able to make such a decision and be fulfilled herself also involves some decisions and actions by the father in the home. We'll save that for the next chapter.

Still another reason that it is harder than ever to be a mother today is the tremendous gap in the values between youth and adults. The generation problem is more awesome than in earlier times because three radical reversals in values have occurred. Youth today are convinced that people are more important than property. Jesus taught this and lived it. We have copied him with lip service, but in fact property values have come first in the long run. To the adult, nothing is more important than his savings, his car, his house, his land, and the buildings he builds such as churches, banks, and universities. We say the key to fine character is hard work, thrift, and responsibleness because by these we gain wealth and property. From English common law to our present legal codes, all is based on property rights.

Suddenly we have a generation growing up in our homes saying that property is not all that important and that real value is in human relationships, caring, and loving. Our children have dared to defy the law to say that building is evil; our sons have not marched out to conquer the business world but to "waste themselves" in school and humanitarian projects.

A second new value our youth are springing on us is that the future is more important than the past. We know we are on a raft floating in space, living in a global village. They know that America is an island of affluence in a sea of misery. They know that traditions, old loyalties, and corporate profits have to be set aside to stop waste and pollution. They know that somehow, someway, and sometime soon the wealth of the world has to be more evenly distributed because life or death hangs in the balance. The future, they know, is theirs, and they are no longer safely separated from dangers by time or geography. Our neighbor is not only on the other side of the earth; he is also the unborn child. The values of love and caring for people do not mean only for those near us and like us, say these youth. Nationalism is outdated because nations and the split atom cannot exist in the same world. The future is more important than the past, and we have a greater obligation to it than to the past. It sounds wonderfully like Jesus, who lives not only behind us in history but before us in history, and who calls us to new life in his Kingdom.

The third reversal of values is that children today are wiser than their fathers. In the past, the elders knew more than the children and the children built upon what the elders taught them. Today the frequent doubling of all accumulated knowledge, nuclear energy, and advances in communications have swept us into a radically new dimension. No elders alive know what their children know. I do not mean intellectually but emotionally. Those of us born before 1945 cannot know the visceral experience of those

born after that watershed of history, the atomic age. I am
speaking as a father, born in 1928. Those depression years
had their traumas, but the family was thrown together and
emotionally there was stability. Our children know nothing
of our pre–World War II life, nothing of stability and peace.
They are at home in turmoil, having never known a day that
Doom was not hanging over their heads.

No wonder parents are bewildered by children who are
so different from what they were themselves! How uncer-
tain and helpless a mother feels in all of this, trying to tell
the children what is right and no longer being sure herself!
It is the children who now tell the parents what is right. The
reality of war, pollution, hunger, poverty, and death are
close to this generation and they are affected by them as we
never were. We could be isolated, they cannot be. They are
wiser than their parents not only in their experience of this
new world situation but in the insight that much of our
society must begin all over. They have accepted the fact that
there is no safe road to travel because they never imagined
they had an alternative. They know that the possible solu-
tions do not lie in the ways socially approved by their parents. These young people are at home in the midst of
change because nothing is increasing at a faster rate.

We adults can hardly cope with these new facts and values. Our answer is to trust in the Christ who is still the
pioneer. He allows us not to be afraid of our feelings. We
long to feel something so we can believe it "in our guts,"
so we can have assurance, know it's real! Adults today are
crying out for a religious experience, an experience of God,
that blasts through all the confusion and monstrosities. They
have not been able to know this reality because they have
so bottled up their feelings. Our youth are having a spiritual

revival because they allow themselves to feel. They are expressing themselves instead of repressing it all as their parents often do.

It is trust in Jesus that will allow us to listen to the youth in our homes and hear their heartbeats. We have put them under the terrible pressure of our own uncertainties and shaky relationships. The apocalyptic possibility of the bomb or ecological disaster is always there. We press for the best grades possible in school, and sign them up for lessons and activities, because it is performance that counts with us. We imply that if they do well we will love them more, yet these children most of all need someone to affirm that they are loved for themselves alone, not because of how they perform. It is being a person that counts, not being smart or dumb, clean or dirty, green or orange. It is Jesus who will fill us adults with love, free us from our defensiveness, turn us from the idols of pride and production, and enable us to listen to this new generation.

To be *present* with another is the sign of love. It is harder than it's ever been for a mother to do that with her family, unless she allows Christ to fill her with his Spirit.

One Easter vacation Ruth and I lived with twelve teenagers in our mountain home. The routine included several hours each day just listening to one another as we sat round the fireplace. Two of our own children were in the group and the interaction among us all was full of new discoveries. One thing the young people discovered was that parents are people too, with needs to be met. They realized that youth must listen to their parents; not just their lectures, but to their heart hungers as well.

As we listened we also discovered how often we misinterpret our children because we assume their reaction to life is the same as ours. Believe it or not, it is a new day. Being a mother is harder than it ever was, but that situation is also loaded with the potential for greater rewards and joys than ever before.

Chapter 14

How Father Fits In

The missionary Elizabeth Elliott tells how the earliest memory of her father was his absence. He had gone on a long trip and the children were home with their mother. It was the only time Elizabeth saw her mother cry when they were young. She remembers the feeling of danger during an electrical storm. It wasn't really the storm that frightened her, but the knowledge that her father was gone. She remembers the endless weeks he was away, and then the rapture of waking up one morning to find he had returned. She recalls the security of his routine: going to the office each morning, then home just before six each evening, opening the front door and giving the chickadee call that was his signal to her mother. Then the supper together each night at which father asked the blessing and served the plates and talked to them about his work. She remembers the discussions on Christian concerns. She remembers the Bible-readings after the meal and sometimes the horseplay on the living room floor later in the evening. She recalls the walks they would take together on Saturday afternoons and the Hershey bars that miraculously would be found in the bushes.

She never thought of him as a "pal"; always as a father, and a little awesome. She never doubted his authority. He said what he meant. Of course he made mistakes. She recalls his temper, which would flare; and he would stamp around the house and slam doors, for which he sometimes apologized. She says, however, that none of his mistakes was as serious as the one he did *not* make—that of *not* being a father! (*Christianity Today,* June 18, 1971, p. 3.)

A verse from Ephesians comes to mind: "Fathers, do not provoke your children to anger, but bring them up in the discipline and instruction of the Lord" (Eph. 6:4). When I took on the role of fatherhood I had not yet found that verse. "Fathers, do not provoke your children to anger." A child's first encounter with God is in his father. To the child, father seems to be omnipotent, omniscient, and omnipresent. Just look at what father can do: fix dolls and bikes, dole out allowances and Sunday school offerings, wield occasional belts, banish nightmarish ghosts, explain the fine points of football, chase boyfriends home after hours, face family crises, and comfort broken hearts. Fathers finance record collections, summer vacations, wardrobes, automobiles, college years. My father used to bewilder me with his knowledge of what I was thinking and doing when I was out of his sight. I remember his telling me over and again, "Well, it wasn't very long ago that I was where you are." I could not grasp that "time" relationship. My father certainly knew that maturity had no shortcuts. He could not walk or run or live for me. But he could love me and suffer with me and set the example for me.

Father is in fact the first "God" we know. And when we become fathers there is no way to avoid this. We are gods to our children. The danger of this is huge because the child soon discovers father has weaknesses, faults, and ignorance. The child then looks for another God and transfers these attributes of omnipotence, omniscience, and omnipresence to the heavenly Father—to whom they really belong. The trouble is that the child also projects onto the heavenly God the mental picture of the earthly father. This causes a crisis of doubt. "What? Trust him? I was let down by my first god. I now live in fear of being let down by my heavenly God."

The answer to this problem is not to run away from the role of father but to live it! Accept the fact that you are God to that child and be the image of God as you know him in Jesus Christ. The Christian experience has everything to do with moving toward that image. Then gently, as the years go by, point the child beyond yourself to the Lord Jesus Christ, who is the perfect image of the invisible God. By the time your child discovers that you are a failure as God, he or she will also be looking beyond you in the direction you are looking, moving with you in the direction that you are moving, and trusting with you in the Lord whom you trust.

The Old Testament patriarchs powerfully fulfilled this role of father. In their strength the children discovered God's strength. One of the Bible's most powerful scenes is the day when Abraham took his only son Isaac on the three-day journey to Mt. Moriah to make a sacrifice to God. It was a primitive day in many ways and human sacrifice was still practiced at times. All of Abraham's hope for the future, all of God's promises and covenant, were embodied in this only son, Isaac. Yet Abraham was convinced that God wanted this child of the promise. What a struggle that father went through! Yet he believed above all else that God's word was sure. God does not lie! If Abraham would be faithful to him, God would keep his promise. No wonder Abraham is called the Father of the Faithful!

The significance of the occasion was only beginning to dawn on the boy Isaac. He carried the fuel for the fire and Abraham carried the torch and the knife. "My father," Isaac said, ". . . behold, the fire and the wood; but where is the lamb for a burnt offering?" Abraham answers, "God will

provide himself the lamb for a burnt offering" (Gen. 22:
7–8). And he did! A ram was caught by its horns in the
thicket. But not until that father had bound his son,
stretched forth his hand, and taken the knife to slay him, not
until the faith of Abraham was completely demonstrated,
did the voice of God break through the dreadful silence.
"Abraham! . . . Do not lay your hand on the lad or do
anything to him; for now I know that you fear God, seeing
you have not withheld your son, your only son, from me."
(Gen. 22:11–12.)

Isaac caught that trust in God from his father and passed
it on to Jacob his son, who passed it on to his twelve sons
who became the tribes of Israel. In time that faith, passed
on and nurtured, found its climax on that same mountain
where Abraham offered Isaac. It became the site of Jerusalem. There another son became the lamb for sacrifice. Trusting in the Father, God, he died saying, "Father, into thy
hands I commit my spirit!" (Luke 23:46).

"Fathers, do not provoke your children to anger, but
bring them up in the discipline and instruction of the Lord."
Most scholars agree that the human family is the most ancient and natural order of society. Husband and wife are
subjectively involved with each other, but when children
come into the family, the family becomes a community and
there is an objective expression to love. These human children, unlike animal babies, need years of loving care in
order to survive. So the family as a stable community has
been a necessity from the beginning. The form of the family
varies from time to time and place to place. But basically
children have developed economically, emotionally, and
intellectually on the instruction of the fathers. It was necessary for survival that they be obedient and respect the father
as their sovereign lord. In the days when family units were

weak, the role of the father was taken over by feudal lords, by national kings, or by religious priests. Now we have come to a day like that again. Our families are weak and the role of the father is being taken over by a benevolent government who is the disciplinarian, the provider, and the educator.

The role of the father in our day is played down. He becomes the stumbling buffoon of the television show who provokes laughs as he tries to keep up with the rest of the family. You know how the series go. He may be the breadwinner, but he is befuddled by the problems of the family. He avoids them by becoming an ogre, or the dancing bear who is manipulated by his clever wife and brilliant children. Who wants a role like that? Men today can see themselves as brothers, buddies, lovers, and husbands, but who takes seriously the role of father? Yet where are children going to learn the discipline and instruction of the Lord if they do not get it from mom and dad, and especially dad, this mysterious figure who so influences his child's experience of God, even by his absence?

One of the finest chapters I can recommend to fathers is from Keith Miller's book *A Second Touch*. Chapter 3 is called "Communicating a Living Faith to One's Own Children— An Uncharted Sea." He makes it clear that being a Christian father is not a matter of formal, pious duties like family devotions or planned playtimes with the children. He tells how he had tried it this way until finally one of his girls came to her mother and said, "Do we *have* to play with daddy any more today?"

Rather, being a Christian father has everything to do with appreciating and cultivating each child as an individual, separate personality, letting the children be with you in the things that you are doing, giving them attention so they know you take them seriously, being free and natural as you share with them not only your successes but your failures and your growing relationship with God. For example, the Miller family always tucked their children in with a standard prayer ritual: "Now I lay me down to sleep" followed by the "God blesses." One night as Keith Miller was going through this with one of their daughters he realized that he was not actually praying with her. Instead he was trying to put words in her mouth and teach her to pray. It dawned on him that none of his children had ever heard their father make any real confession or petition about the things that were real in his life.

The next evening he was cross at the dinner table and glowered at their mother during the meal. Later on as he lay on their five-year-old daughter's bed for prayer time he prayed, "Dear God, forgive me for being fussy at dinner tonight." There followed a kind of awed silence. Then very quickly she went through the familiar prayer.

The next night it just happened, maybe on purpose, that he was also cross at dinner. Again at bedtime prayers this father said, "Dear Lord, forgive me for being cross at dinner again tonight and help me not to be fussy again. I really don't want to be that way. Please help me to try hard not to be." There was the same silence. Then with eyes clenched shut his little girl said, "Dear God, forgive me for teeteeing out in the back yard under the big tree last summer."

Keith writes that he almost laughed and cried at the same time. This was real prayer and real confession. This was her own, not a formal routine! She was learning by example to talk with God about things she could understand—everyday things which are the building blocks to a lifelong trust in God. (Keith Miller, *A Second Touch,* pp. 37ff.; Word Books,

Publisher, 1972. Used by permission of the publisher.)

Not all fathers have communicated this kind of trust to their children. Too many fathers have provoked their children to a deep-seated anger at life. There are fathers who project their hostility and authoritarianism, sometimes even their brutality, on their children. How difficult it is for those children to believe in the heavenly Father. Instead, they may feel rejected by God, and if the matter is not resolved, the resulting anger may prevent them from ever believing in the goodness of God. I meet many angry people who have never resolved their anger toward their parents and are busy projecting it on everybody else, including their children. I would add a verse to Paul's excellent advice in the sixth chapter of Ephesians. It would be this: "Children, let go of the anger provoked by your fathers."

It is a great breakthrough to be able to allow your father to be himself. It is a joy-filled moment when you fashion your understanding of God around the Christ of the New Testament and not around the father in your home. If your father did not help you to make that transfer of trust and loyalty, then it is hoped that you will discover it now. Sometimes it requires some serious psychological counseling to separate all of this out. You may need to learn how to trust in some human being before you can transfer that trust to God. Like a cripple learning to walk again, you may have to learn how to trust again. It is all too easy to go through life blaming dad for our emotional problems. The Hebrews had a proverb that said, "The fathers have eaten sour grapes, and the children's teeth are set on edge." The prophet Jeremiah saw the weakness of this and told them not to use that proverb anymore. He said, "But every one shall die for his own sin; each man who eats sour grapes, his teeth shall be set on edge" (Jer. 31:30).

Ralph Osborne tells how well he remembered his father (*Faith at Work,* December, 1972). He remembered the times his father failed to be available when he needed him. He remembered the negative responses to calls for help. Oh, he remembered his father all right, and it hurt. Then the day arrived when dad, now in his eighties, became critically ill. A phone call informed Ralph that if he wanted to see his father he'd better come right away. For a few minutes recognition came to the father's eyes, although conversation was impossible. Then the empty gaze, and recognition no more.

Ralph began to review the storehouse of memories as he sat beside that bed. There were more memories than he had realized. There were things that had seemed so unimportant: the shape of dad's old brown hat; the glowing tip of his cigarette; the Saturday evening walks to the drugstore for an ice cream cone; the nonproductive attempt to tell his son the facts of life. Long forgotten bits of data began to surface. The Boy Scout hikes they had shared and his dad eating those pancakes as if he really liked them, gluey blobs of glop in the middle, well-charred around the edges. His father had really cared, had taken time just for him. Where had they lost each other through the years?

The depression days of the thirties began to surface in Ralph's memory. His father wasn't there very much during the depression. He remembered two or three scenes, however, from those years. One was the time they went down to the bank together to pay off dad's loan with two hundred dollars Ralph had inherited from his grandmother. Later, the time he visited his father on the road. Dad had gotten a job selling glass jars and had to be away from the family, moving wherever he could find an honest dollar. One more memory: Dad's WPA job had folded and at age seventeen Ralph had gotten a job as an office boy. He was the bread-winner now. There is the memory of that moment in the tenement apartment where he reminds mom and dad that they no longer have control over him. He is a free man.

Now beside this dying man's bed, Ralph begins to see his father from another point of view. Searching through the evidence of those memories he asked himself, "What did he feel like when at seventeen his son began to support the family?" The feelings of his father's aches and personal failures overwhelmed Ralph. Suddenly he realized that he had lost his dad when the grindings of those depression days killed his father's self-respect.

As the hours at that bedside ticked on, Ralph Osborn tells how the relationship between father and son was reestablished. He could no longer tell his father what he thought, nor ask him about those long-gone days. Instead, he wrote him a letter that he would never read, and trusted God to interpret the too-late words to the father who had cared and loved him very much. He wrote, "I know full well now that you did the best you could by me. You did love me, I know, in your own unique . . . way. And I am here to bless you in ways you might not understand: to bless you and let you be yourself, and not some image of what I wanted you to be. I set you free in His peace, entrusted into the love and care of God, whose gracious loving kindness I know far better than His judgement.

"And it's okay, Dad; it's all okay . . . the past, this weary-ing present, and the eternal future.

"Yours, very gratefully,

"Tad."   (*Ibid.,* p. 12; used by permission.)

"Fathers, do not provoke your children to anger, but bring them up in the discipline and instruction of the Lord." Children, let go of your anger for your fathers that they have provoked, and set them free in the love and care of God who is the Father of us all!

Chapter 15

The Prodigal Family

Every week in America more than ten thousand children run away. In one year six hundred thousand minors ran away from home, and experts say that the situation shows little sign of change. Most of the children are between thirteen and seventeen years of age. At first it was thought that this runaway tide would recede when the youth revolt of recent years began to wane. Now it has become apparent that adolescents continue to run at a rate of over half a million a year, and these youngsters are going to be a national problem for some years to come.

In one of his best-known parables Jesus told about one of these runaways. It is a drama that touches the hearts of all of us at some point. Perhaps it gathers up all we have been trying to say about the love that is the basis of God's plan for marriage and home life. Any member of the family who runs away deeply affects all the others. We may run away in the literal sense, but more often we just run away emotionally, spiritually, or intellectually, and leave the others behind. When such a crisis comes to a family, how can it be creatively handled?

It will be helpful, perhaps, to put the ancient story of Luke 15:11–32 into middle-class American idiom and tell it again. It is played out in four scenes.

The first scene is called "The Parting." "Once there was a man who had two sons. The younger one said to his father,

'Father, give me my share of the property that will come to me.' So he divided up his property between the two of them. Before very long, the younger son collected all his belongings and went off to a foreign land, where he squandered his wealth in the wildest extravagance.'' (Phillips.)

This younger son had always been in the shadow of others. It was assumed in the family that the older brother would follow in his father's footsteps and take over the business. But where did this younger boy fit in? As high school wore on he became more and more confused. What was the meaning of his life? The curriculum at school did not answer that question, but the question still burned in his heart. He desperately needed to establish an identity that was his own. The treadmill of social success and conformity to adult ideas was simply unacceptable to him. Even his church seemed irrelevant. People were talking about love but isolating themselves from those who were hurting and who needed love the most. Nothing inspiring about that! He looked around and saw others breaking loose: playboys, liberated women, angry ethnics, street people. It was the street people who intrigued him the most, with their underground network, their primitive life-style, their tribal poverty and free love. The more he compared this with what the adults had to offer, the more he wanted to experience the intense feelings of life. His friends called it being "turned on."

At first he became an imitator and played at it. He went slumming, wore the symbols, and talked the language, but it was make-believe. Later he became a fellow traveler. He was developing a philosophy now. He found that many of these rebels were attractive, intelligent people. He began dropping out a day at a time, wandering in the city park and feeling good about the way others he met accepted him. At last he decided to become one of them, a committed street person. He would go into neutral. He would cut loose from the establishment.

One day he appeared in his father's office to announce his decision. The father knew that it would do no good to argue. This decision had been building up for a long time. It had become impossible even to have the boy around. The father could have cut him off, told him to get out and stay out, but the image of the father is God in the story that Jesus told. We human parents are inconsistent. We have so often failed our children. We too are prodigal and need repentance. But God doesn't reject his children. They cut themselves off from him and he gives them that freedom. So the father in the story allows the boy the freedom to decide. Real sonship is of the heart and soul and will. This boy only play-acted at being a son. Better let him go.

"Father, give me what you would spend on me in college!" Well, that's at least twelve thousand dollars today. Dad didn't have that kind of cash, so he went to the bank and mortgaged the house to get the money for the boy. Any counselor will tell you that the kid will hang himself on a rope like that. The boy had no right to that money. But God gives us all the freedom we need to hang ourselves. There weren't many words exchanged. The father just drove him out to the edge of town and dropped him off on the highway. They shook hands and the boy said, "Now, Dad, don't worry about me! I'm going to really live. Later on I'll settle down to become a writer and you are going to be proud of me. You just wait." Only then did the father speak. He said, "Just remember, Son, you can always come home."

Back home, after he had broken the news to the boy's mother, they sat together in the afternoon silence. They looked around the house and remembered the years their youngster had grown up, the family holidays together, the bright-eyed questions of childhood, the adolescent turmoils, and how helpless they had felt in trying to break through to him. The gap of misunderstanding had grown wider and wider. They walked arm in arm back to their son's room. There on the walls were the pictures, his school shoes were by the bed, his fishing pole hung in the corner. His hobbies were still on the shelves, his desk still littered with papers from school. The father turned to the mother and he said, "Now, let's shut the door and just leave it like it is. He'll be back one of these days!"

The second scene is called "The Squandering": "And when he had run through all his money, a terrible famine arose in that country, and he began to feel the pinch. Then he went and hired himself out to one of the citizens of that country who sent him out into the fields to feed the pigs. He got to the point of longing to stuff himself with the food the pigs were eating, and not a soul gave him anything." (Phillips.) We follow the boy as he heads for the city with enough money to last him for years. He put it in a checking account and bought himself a pad of paper so he could start his writing. Soon he was in the big city park, and the air was filled with the smell of dope. He smiled at the thought of "really living." He threw up his arms and ran to the sound of ankle bells and the hypnotic beat of bongo drums. Clusters of young people were here and there smoking marijuana. It seemed so good to have people come by and say, "I love you."

Soon he learned that everyone shares everything. Many would ask for rent money and he gave it freely. He found a community of writers and he shared their pad, a messy floor in a tenement. The days began to blur namelessly into one another. All sense of time was gone. He became absorbed in the life of trying to experience each moment by itself. The past and the future were shut out. There was always music so loud that it stunned the mind and set the nerve fibers twitching. The continuous rhythm caught up the body and soul in abandonment. He kept meeting people who were hungry and evicted. As he paid their way he would be taken in to live in their communal tribe. The drugs cost more and more but while he was on trips he thought he could feel reality. He felt holy, at one with the universe. When the drugs wore off he was unable to re-create that effect alone. There were those moments when he allowed himself to think and he realized the big question had not yet been answered for him: What is the purpose of life? And who was he? There was some purpose in giving away what you had to help others, but now he didn't have anything left to give. The best part was the feeling of joy and love and identity with everything. You could get this feeling through drugs or chanting and music, and through sex. But always it would be over, and then where did you go? Some went on to higher and higher kicks, but the powerful chemicals were blowing their minds and they ended up as walking vegetables.

The months passed and the money was gone. He was begging like the others now. He lived in a filthy, litter-strewn dope house. Hepatitis and syphilis were rampant. In every room there were blank-faced males and females who lay in drugged stupors or swayed to the blaring rock music. The flies swarmed through the marijuana smoke and when he would wake up there would be people all around him shooting their veins or talking in a whirling falsetto or thrashing on the floor as they freaked out. The Phillips translation describes this moment clearly. "Then he came to his senses and cried aloud, 'Why, dozens of my father's hired men have got more food than they can eat, and here am I dying of hunger! I will get up and go back to my father, and I will say to him: 'Father, I have done wrong in the sight of Heaven and in your eyes. I don't deserve to be called your son any more. Please take me on as one of your hired men.' " That doesn't need any new interpretation. No one is so lost, so mixed up, so low that he cannot come to his senses and decide to change the situation.

He looked around him and remembered the warmth of home, the cleanness, the love . . . the father's love! Love is the greatest pulling power in the world. What had he done to those who love him? Here he was saying, "I love you," to these people who lived only for themselves while breaking the hearts of that mother and dad who needed him above all else. Right there, in that moment, he saw the lie of it. Self-indulgence as the goal of life is a lie! Anarchy never brings fulfillment whether in society or economics or politics or lovemaking. He had been told to go "do his own bag." Everybody had his "bag"! That turned out to be a very small package. This runaway had "his bag" over his head and he was suffocating. For him to feel good at the expense of society was just as impossible as the establishment that he had rejected. This way of life had no answers, no relevance, no purpose. He gave up material things, but that was all for kicks. Real sacrifice is giving up the self. If he would do that he didn't have to be trapped by the system. He could change the system. There's a cause to really turn you on! The real turn-on to life is when you discover servanthood! "Please take me on as one of your hired men." This is the key to our identity crisis: become servants of the God and Father of Jesus Christ. Then you will know who you are and where you are going!

The third scene is the "Homecoming." "He got up and

went to his father." You can do that, you know. There is always this when everything else is hopeless. Here the father in the story takes on the character of God. He is not like our earthly fathers, prodigal in their own way. He is the ultimate Father, the Father of Jesus—not the God of nature who is Power; not the God of science who is Reason. Those are facets of God's greatness, but you don't come home and fall into the arms of power and reason. This is why we need Jesus. He brings us home to the Father. He is the image of the invisible God who turns out to *be* the Father! So the boy went out on the highway and started hitchhiking home. It wasn't as romantic as it was the first time. He was afraid now. He was a failure and felt guilty. He wasn't returning home in a blaze of glory, a noted author, as he had imagined.

"But while he was still some distance off, his father saw him and his heart went out to him, and he ran and fell on his neck and kissed him." (Phillips.) Did the father just happen to see the boy coming? No, he had been going out onto the highways at night and looking into the faces of the hitchhikers. He went up to San Francisco once and walked the streets, longing and looking and asking, but there was no sign of the boy. He had prayed a thousand prayers. In his office, in the middle of the day, a wave of sorrow would come over him and he would put his head down on his papers and weep. Every time a bus went by he searched the windows for a glimpse of what might be the boy coming home. Then it happened! One evening as that father was out in front watering the grass, down the street the boy came, dirty and smelly and sick, with a scraggly beard. The father spotted him half a block down and dropped the hose still spouting all over the grass. He ran down the street. Who cared what the neighbors thought! Did he tell the boy to go

on in and wash and clean up and shave and then they'd sit
down and talk this thing over? No, he just fell on him and
hugged him and kissed him, dirt and all. And the boy kept
trying to get out his prepared speech. He'd worked on that
speech for days: "Dad, I'm no good. I'm not worth being
your son. I'll live in a rooming house somewhere. Just give
me a job in your office as a hired hand." But he never got
his speech out. It was smothered in the arms of the father.
The boy hardly knew what happened, but there they were
running together down the street, and the father calling,
"Mother, thaw out the roast for Sunday, air out his room,
lay out those good clothes, turn on the music, and call the
family! Our son whom we thought was dead, is alive! He
has come home!"

I wish Jesus had ended the parable there, but he goes on
with one more scene, "The Brothering." Emotionally this
is an anticlimax. We are reminded of the older brother. He
had never been involved in the life of this younger brother
of his, and suddenly he has to acknowledge that he has a
brother. He doesn't like it. It pinches; there's no room!
He'd always accused this kid brother of being spoiled and
now this proved it. He had stayed at home and worked
while the kid went out and tasted all the sensual kicks that
the elder brother wanted but had chosen to avoid. The kid
had put the whole family into debt, and now he was back,
broke, dishonoring everyone, horning in on things. Well,
if he had poverty that was his problem. Leave him in it. If
he wants a job, let him get one. But leave the elder brother
out of it!

He wouldn't even come in, but hid out in the garage.
While the younger brother was showering, the father went
out to the garage to talk to the older boy. The hardest part
of all is getting brothers to accept each other as the father

accepts them. Jesus leaves the story open. Would they become reconciled? We don't know. What happened next would decide whether that home would be a heaven of love or a hell of strife. The older son could also break the father's heart by never being reconciled to his brother. We don't have to run off and be rebels to break the heart of God. We can do that right in church or in our nice, clean homes. We don't have to be runaways or failures. Elder brothers who stay at home are also prodigals who need to repent. Many of us in our homes are prodigal families. Many congregations have been prodigal families. Often a community is a prodigal family. This nation and this world of nations is a prodigal family. There will be no Kingdom of God, no salvation, until we are reconciled.

Do you know what it takes to be reconciled? It takes conversion, a turning around, a changed way of life. This world is going to burn with the fires of hatred until our hearts burn with the fires of Christ's love. This comes not by winning your point, not by trying to establish who is wrong, but by surrender to the power of Jesus, who drives you out of yourself and into the arms of the one you have despised, avoided, and ignored. That's where Jesus leaves it. The next move is yours.